DRUMMER'S GUIDE TO ODD TIME SIGNATURES

RICK LANDWEHR

Alfred, the leader in educational music publishing,

and the National Guitar Workshop,

one of America's finest guitar schools, have joined

forces to bring you the best, most progressive

educational tools possible. We hope you will enjoy

this book and encourage you to look for

other fine products from Alfred and the

National Guitar Workshop.

Alfred Music Publishing Co., Inc.
P.O. Box 10003
Van Nuys, CA 91410-0003
alfred.com

ISBN-10: 0-7390-6539-4 (Book & CD)
ISBN-13: 978-0-7390-6539-6 (Book & CD)

*This book was acquired, edited, and produced
by Workshop Arts, Inc., the publishing arm of
the National Guitar Workshop.
Nathaniel Gunod, acquisitions, managing editor
Burgess Speed, acquisitions, senior editor
Timothy Phelps, interior design
Ante Gelo, music typesetter
CD recorded by Collin Tilton at Bar None Studio, Northford, CT
Rick Landwehr, drums*

*Cover photograph:
drummer boy © Arthur Carlo Franco / iStockphoto*

CONTENTS

ABOUT THE AUTHOR

PHOTO BY WARREN BIRD

Rick Landwehr began playing drums in 1983. He is a graduate of Berklee College of Music and has studied privately with Tom Twiss, Gerald Cleaver, Jim Chapin, Dave Weigert, Gary Chaffee, and Casey Scheuerell.

Rick is a faculty member of the National Guitar Workshop, where he has performed with guest artists like Gary Hoey and Vernon Reid. He has performed and recorded with several groups including Tamandua, Ra Quintet, Daniel Bennett Group, Colin Stack and Novelty Act, and Cirkestra. With Daniel Bennett Group, he has shared the stage with Bill Frisell, Charlie Hunter, and James Carter. Rick is also the percussionist on the soundtrack to the film *Darkon*.

Rick endorses Vic Firth products, Evans drum heads, and Puresound snare drum wires.

For more about Rick and his music, please visit: www.ricklandwehr.com

ACKNOWLEDGEMENTS

Rick would like to thank his family and friends who supported his choice to pursue music as a career. He would also like to thank Burgess Speed at Workshop Arts for his assistance with this book and Collin Tilton at Bar None Studio for recording the accompanying CD.

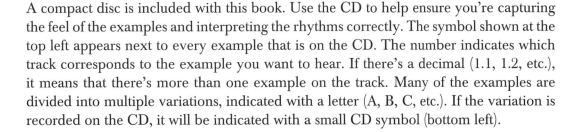

A compact disc is included with this book. Use the CD to help ensure you're capturing the feel of the examples and interpreting the rhythms correctly. The symbol shown at the top left appears next to every example that is on the CD. The number indicates which track corresponds to the example you want to hear. If there's a decimal (1.1, 1.2, etc.), it means that there's more than one example on the track. Many of the examples are divided into multiple variations, indicated with a letter (A, B, C, etc.). If the variation is recorded on the CD, it will be indicated with a small CD symbol (bottom left).

INTRODUCTION

Odd time signatures are, simply, time signatures with an odd number of beats to the bar. (The word "odd" does not mean they are "weird" time signatures.) The purpose of this book is to help drummers gain a better understanding of how to feel, hear, and understand odd time signatures, and how to apply these concepts to different musical situations and styles. You will develop these skills by gaining an understanding of (and eventually internalizing) the concepts of "pulse," "subdivisions," and "note groupings" (explained in Chapter Two). Odd time signatures are quite common in the music of many cultures. They can be found in Balkan music, eastern European and Middle Eastern music, and are becoming more and more common in American/western European popular music and jazz. In fact, these time signatures have been finding their way into "contemporary" music for several decades now. The Beatles used odd time signatures regularly (one example is the song "All You Need Is Love," with verses in $\frac{7}{4}$ time). The Dave Brubeck Quartet's "Take Five" (in $\frac{5}{4}$ time) was a hit single in the late 1950s. One of the most common time signatures, $\frac{3}{4}$, or "waltz" time, is an odd time signature. Almost anyone who has played in a school band is familiar with this meter. Many songs for children are in $\frac{3}{4}$ as well. Popular and influential artists like Radiohead, Tool, Metallica, Soundgarden, Sting, Genesis, Peter Gabriel, Yes, and King Crimson have used odd time signatures to varying degrees.

As these time signatures become more and more common, it is important for musicians to become familiar with them. The more gigs you get, the higher the possibility that you will be called upon to play in these time signatures. This book will help you understand and apply odd time signatures. You'll see that odd time signatures are not difficult, they are just different from $\frac{4}{4}$. Don't psych yourself out with negative thoughts—while attending a Bulgarian wedding music performance, I witnessed a room full of people, who were not musicians, dancing in what might be referred to as $\frac{11}{16}$. They knew the tune to which they were dancing and never thought twice about what time signature it was in!

This book is intended for intermediate and advanced drummers who have a good grasp of the basics and wish to broaden their musical vocabulary. Before getting into any chapter that addresses odd time variations of a style with which you are unfamiliar (rock, jazz, Brazilian, Afro-Cuban, etc.), it is strongly recommended that you investigate the more traditional concepts and techniques of that style by working with a private teacher, listening to recordings, attending live performances, and using method books.

PRACTICE TIPS

The exercises in this book should be practiced slowly at first. You should count them out, then repeat them without counting, until you are comfortable. This will help you internalize the rhythms so you will not have to rely on counting when you play (counting to "11" at a fast tempo is not particularly conducive to performing in a loose, relaxed manner). Once you become comfortable with these rhythms, you can gradually increase the tempo. Trying to play too fast too soon will only be a waste of time because you will just be practicing to play sloppily. At the beginning of each example is a *tempo marking* (for example: ♩ = 110, which means there are 110 quarter notes per minute). The tempo markings in this book represent the performance speed of the examples on the accompanying CD; they do not necessarily indicate the "correct" tempos. The goal is to be able to play the examples at several different tempos with a relaxed, musical feel. On the accompanying CD, most of the examples are repeated four times, but you can repeat them as many times as it takes to feel comfortable.

CHAPTER ONE
NOTATION REVIEW

DRUMSET NOTATION KEY

The following notation key shows how the different parts of the drumset appear on the musical staff throughout this book.

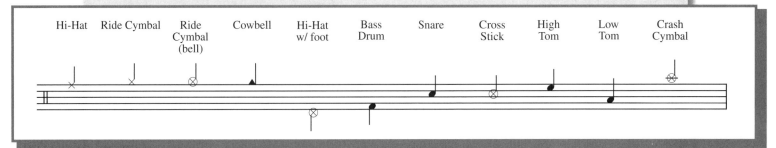

NOTE VALUES

Following are the basic note *values* (durations) in 4/4 time (see Time Signatures on the next page). Under each staff, you will see how these note values can be counted.

RESTS

A *rest* indicates silence. For each note value, there is a corresponding rest value.

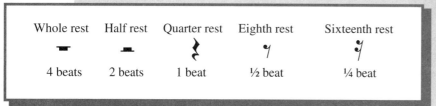

Whole rest	Half rest	Quarter rest	Eighth rest	Sixteenth rest
4 beats	2 beats	1 beat	½ beat	¼ beat

DOTTED NOTES

When a *dot* is placed to the right of a notehead (or rest), it means that one half the value is added to that note (or rest). For example, a dotted quarter note has the duration of one-and-a-half quarter notes (three eighth notes). A dotted eighth note has the duration of one-and-a-half eighth notes (three sixteenth notes).

Count: 1   2   &   3   4   &

Count: 1 e & a 2 e & a 3 e & a 4 e & a

MEASURES

Beats are the most basic unit of musical time. They are grouped into *measures,* or *bars,* of equal length—that is, each measure contains the same number of beats. Measures are marked with vertical *barlines.* Short sections end with a *double barline.*

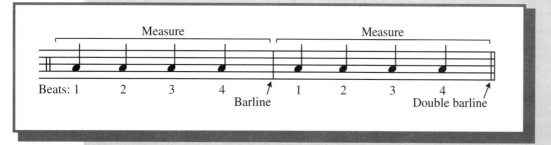

TIME SIGNATURES

A *time signature* is found at the beginning of each piece of music. It indicates how many beats are in each measure and what type of note receives one beat.

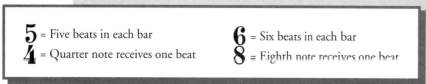

5 = Five beats in each bar
4 = Quarter note receives one beat

6 = Six beats in each bar
8 = Eighth note receives one beat

SWING EIGHTH NOTES

The concept of *swing eighth notes* can be understood by taking a steady flow of eighth-note triplets and removing the middle note of each triplet. This leaves us with a feeling of eighth notes that are no longer evenly spaced. Swing eighths are usually written as straight eighth notes with an indication such as "Swing 8ths," "Swing," or "Shuffle" in the upper left corner. (In this book, we'll use *Swing 8ths*.) This same concept applies to *swing sixteenth notes*. Take a group of sixteenth-note triplets and remove the middle note of each triplet.

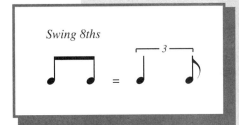

REPEATS

A *repeat sign* tells you to go back to the beginning of the music or to the nearest repeat sign and repeat the section you just played.

A *repeat bar sign* tells you to repeat the measure you just played.

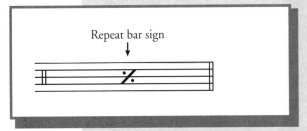

ACCENTS

An accent mark (>) above a note means that note should be played louder than the unaccented notes.

CHAPTER TWO
BUILDING BLOCKS

PULSE, SUBDIVISIONS, AND NOTE GROUPINGS

Throughout this book, we will refer to the concepts of *pulse, subdivisions,* and *note groupings.*

PULSE

On page 6, you learned that the bottom number of a time signature indicates the note value that receives one beat. This is true in theory, but not necessarily always in practice. In time signatures where the quarter note receives the beat ($\frac{4}{4}$, $\frac{5}{4}$, etc.), the basic *pulse* (the "big" note on which the smaller *subdivisions* like eighth notes, sixteenth notes, and eighth-note triplets are based) is the quarter note (see right).

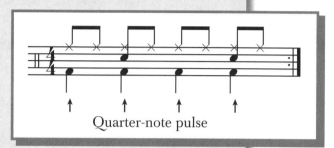
Quarter-note pulse

The basic pulse in a time signature like $\frac{6}{8}$, however, is the dotted quarter note, not the eighth note. This dotted quarter-note pulse is typically subdivided into three eighth notes, six sixteenth notes, or some combination of the two (see right). This gives a feeling of "**1**, 2, 3, **2**, 2, 3" rather than "1, 2, 3, 4, 5, 6."

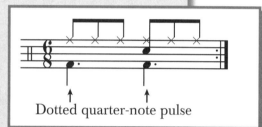
Dotted quarter-note pulse

This concept of quarter-note and dotted quarter-note pulse will become very important later in the book.

SUBDIVISIONS

The concept of subdivisions can refer to two situations:

1. How the basic beat or pulse within a measure of musical time is divided. For example, when quarter notes are subdivided into eighths, sixteenths, or triplets.

2. How the measure itself is divided. For example, one measure of $\frac{4}{4}$ can be subdivided into four quarter-note pulses; and one measure of $\frac{6}{8}$ can be subdivided into two dotted quarter-note pulses.

NOTE GROUPINGS

Note groupings refer to the way in which subdivided beats are grouped together. For example, if you think of a straight-ahead rock beat in $\frac{4}{4}$ time, it can be conceptualized as four groups of two eighth notes (see below).

In the example above, each quarter note is subdivided into two eighth notes. Many of you have probably learned basic eighth-note rock beats, and their variations, by using the count "1-&, 2-&, 3-&, 4-&." This divides the beats into four groups of two eighth notes (which can be further subdivided into four groups of four sixteenth notes counted as "1-e-&-a, 2-e-&-a, 3-e-&-a, 4-e-&-a." A bar of $\frac{4}{4}$ (subdivided as eighth notes) could just as easily be counted "1-2, 2-2, 3-2, 4-2" or "1-2, 1-2, 1-2, 1-2." Keep this in mind for later.

Now, we'll look at a beat in $\frac{12}{8}$, which can be thought of as four groups of three eighth notes.

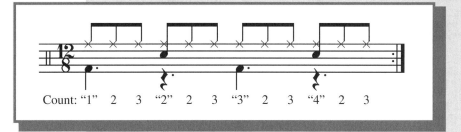

Count: "1" 2 3 "2" 2 3 "3" 2 3 "4" 2 3

This meter is based on a dotted quarter-note pulse, as opposed to a quarter-note pulse. The dotted quarter note subdivides into three eighth notes. $\frac{12}{8}$ time is often counted "1-2-3, 2-2-3, 3-2-3, 4-2-3" or "1-&-a, 2-&-a, 3-&-a, 4-&-a." Another time signature subdivided this way is $\frac{6}{8}$, which is counted "1-2-3, 2-2-3; 1-2-3, 2-2-3" etc.

So, there you have it. Measures break down into groups of two and three notes which create a basic pulse within the measure. The basic pulse of $\frac{4}{4}$ is four quarter notes. The basic pulse of $\frac{12}{8}$ is four dotted quarter notes. This same concept carries over to time signatures such as $\frac{12}{16}$ (which is counted the same way as $\frac{12}{8}$). Four dotted eighth notes (four groups of three sixteenth notes) equal one bar of $\frac{12}{16}$.

RHYTHMIC CELLS

There are only so many different rhythms that can be played on one beat. These one-beat ideas can be considered *rhythmic cells* because they are the basic materials for musical ideas of any length. They combine to create the many variations found in groove patterns, fills, and solos.

Below are some rhythmic cells based on a quarter-note pulse. These cells will be used to create the examples throughout this book.

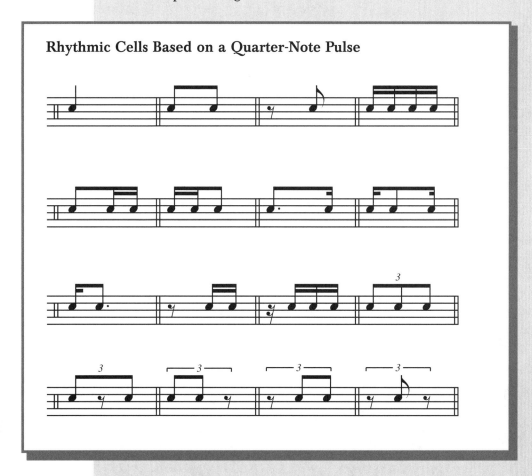

Rhythmic Cells Based on a Quarter-Note Pulse

Below are some rhythmic cells based on a dotted quarter-note pulse.

Rhythmic Cells Based on a Dotted Quarter-Note Pulse

ORCHESTRATION

Orchestration occurs when you move the notes of a rhythm to different parts of the drumset to create melodic variations. A pattern typically played on the snare drum will sound much different if you move your hands to other drums or substitute one of your feet for a note typically played with your hand.

The different combinations and orchestrations of the rhythmic cells produce seemingly endless variations. The examples in this book are meant to increase your overall musical vocabulary and broaden your improvisational skills. It is recommended that you use your creativity to come up with your own rhythmic combinations and orchestrations. You should keep a log of the variations you come up with. Ideally, you will get to a point where you can improvise grooves and fills in odd time signatures just as comfortably as you can in $\frac{4}{4}$ (be patient!). The goal is to be able to react to the music you are playing and come up with musical phrases in real time. Avoid arbitrarily inserting examples from this book into a new odd time song you are learning or rehearsing. Use your ears! The music should ultimately dictate what you play.

CHAPTER THREE
¾ AND ⁶⁄₈ REVIEW

Before we dive into odd time signatures like ⁵⁄₄ and ⁷⁄₄, let's quickly review ¾ and ⁶⁄₈. (Although ⁶⁄₈ is not an odd time signature, it relates to material later in this book.) If you are already comfortable playing in these meters, feel free to skip ahead to the next chapter. Otherwise, this section can serve as a crash course, or review.

¾ is the shortest odd time signature with a quarter-note pulse. It is also the most common odd time signature in Western music. ¾, or waltz time, consists of three quarter notes per bar. It is important to count while practicing in this time signature ("1, 2, 3; 1, 2, 3," etc.) so that you can internalize its feel. A common problem for drummers first playing in "three" is that they unintentionally add a beat, turning it into ⁴⁄₄; this often occurs when improvising fills. ⁴⁄₄ is the most familiar time signature for most of us, so it is no surprise that this happens.

ROCK AND FUNK GROOVES IN ¾

Following are examples of *time-playing patterns* (grooves, or beats) in ¾, incorporating *straight-eighth* and *straight-sixteenth* note subdivisions of the quarter-note pulse. (The terms "straight eighth" and "straight sixteenth" indicate that the swing rhythm is not being used.) More often than not, these straight time-playing patterns will be found in rock, funk, progressive rock, and fusion. These are only some of the possible rhythmic combinations. After you familiarize yourself with the written examples, use your own creativity to come up with more variations. The ultimate goal is to be able to improvise patterns that make musical sense with the melodies and rhythms you are hearing during the course of a musical performance.

Below are some more examples in $\frac{3}{4}$.

JAZZ IN $\frac{3}{4}$

Now, let's move on to jazz time playing in $\frac{3}{4}$. For those of you unfamiliar with jazz time playing, the following examples are not like the "beats," or "grooves," referred to in rock time playing. They are not meant to be repeated over and over again to create a foundation of time. They are intended to help you get comfortable with *comping* (accompaniment). A quick definition of comping could be "the shifting of drum patterns in relationship to time playing on the cymbal, as an accompaniment to an improvised jazz solo." So, instead of playing a repetitive "beat," you are having a real-time musical "conversation" with the soloist and other rhythm section players. It is important to understand that just because jazz time playing does not rely on repeated "beats," you do not have to be overly active. It's okay to leave space and just play simple time. If you listen to Miles Davis's album *Kind of Blue*, you'll hear Jimmy Cobb laying down some great-feeling time with a minimum of busy comping ideas. He could have played more, but chose not to.

We will start with a simple time-playing pattern in $\frac{3}{4}$.

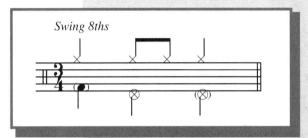

The following examples demonstrate snare drum/bass drum comping ideas against a steady pattern played between the ride cymbal and *stepped hi-hat* (hi-hat played with the foot). All eighth notes should be played as swing eighths. Parentheses around a note indicates that the note is optional. It is recommended that you try to play both of the stepped hi-hat variations suggested in the example above (hi-hat on beat 2, and hi-hat on beats 2 and 3). After you become comfortable with these, try some of your own ride cymbal and stepped hi-hat patterns with the written snare/bass combinations. Also, try moving your snare drum hand around to different drums for more melodic ideas (orchestrations).

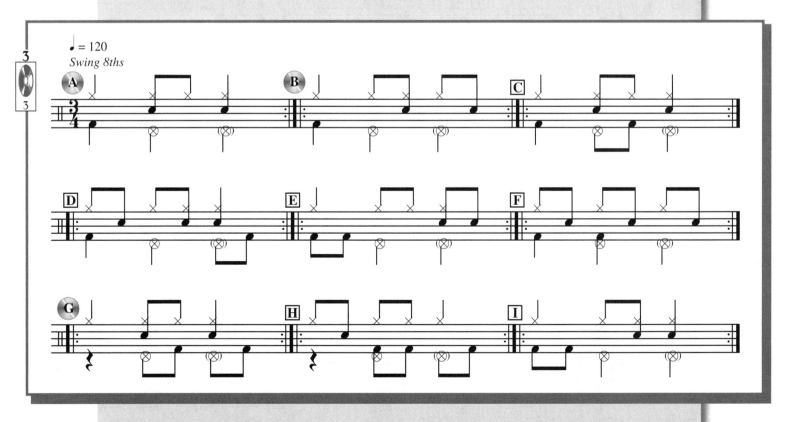

Here are some more jazz examples in $\frac{3}{4}$.

BASIC $\frac{6}{8}$ GROOVES

Remember (page 8), $\frac{6}{8}$ is a time signature with a dotted quarter-note pulse. Each bar subdivides into two groups of three eighth notes. This differs from $\frac{3}{4}$, which subdivides into three groups of two eighth notes. Both time signatures have the same amount of eighth notes per bar, but the different note groupings completely change how each meter feels. Below are some examples of time-playing patterns in $\frac{6}{8}$ time. Remember to count while practicing these patterns to internalize the dotted quarter-note pulse.

Count: 1   2   3   **2**   2   3   etc.

CHAPTER FOUR
TIME PLAYING IN FIVE

PLAYING IN $\frac{5}{4}$

Now, we move on to $\frac{5}{4}$ time playing. In this time signature, the quarter notes in a measure are often divided into groups of two and three (2+3). This feels like a bar of $\frac{2}{4}$ followed by a bar of $\frac{3}{4}$. The count is "1, 2, 1, 2, 3." In this book, note groupings are indicated by a dotted line in the measure. Check out the example below.

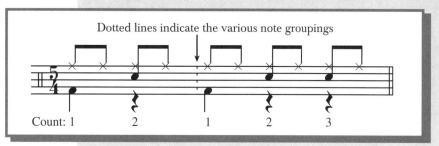

Another way to subdivide $\frac{5}{4}$ is the note grouping 3+2. This feels like a bar of $\frac{3}{4}$ followed by a bar of $\frac{2}{4}$. The count is "1, 2, 3, 1, 2."

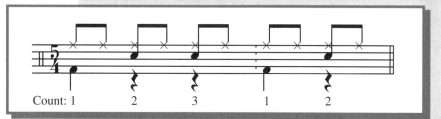

Both of the note groupings above add up to five beats, but they each have a different feel. Subdividing odd time signatures greater than three into smaller units can help you internalize the feel of these meters and will prevent you from stumbling over yourself when trying to count every beat (particularly, in longer time signatures such as $\frac{11}{4}$ and at faster tempos). In the odd time signatures with a constant quarter-note pulse ($\frac{5}{4}$, $\frac{7}{4}$, etc.), the groupings of two and three are not always as clear as the examples above and can sometimes be interpreted in more than one way based on the placement of the snare drum and bass drum. In this book, the examples will be separated by the most strongly suggested subdivision of the bar. For instance, in the example above, the measure starts with a quarter note on the bass drum and is followed by two quarter notes on the snare drum—this would suggest a grouping of three. The remainder of the measure consists of a quarter note on the bass drum followed by a quarter note on the snare—this would suggest a grouping of two. The concept of subdividing bars into twos and threes will have more significance when we get to odd time signatures such as $\frac{5}{8}$ and $\frac{7}{8}$, which do not have a constant quarter-note pulse.

When playing in $\frac{5}{4}$ (or any time signature, for that matter) it is important to listen to the melody, the other rhythm section instruments (bass, rhythm guitar, keyboards), and the chord changes of the composition. This will give you a sense of how to phrase your time playing. Chord changes on the first and third beat of a bar of $\frac{5}{4}$ are a clear indication of a 2+3 subdivision. Do not just insert random $\frac{5}{4}$ "beats" into a composition because it is in $\frac{5}{4}$. Let the music suggest what you play. As mentioned in Chapter Two, the written patterns in this book are here to help you internalize how these time signatures feel. There are many more variations that can be played. Use your imagination to come up with variations of your own.

ROCK AND FUNK GROOVES IN $\frac{5}{4}$

Following are examples of time-playing patterns in $\frac{5}{4}$, incorporating variations of straight-eighth and sixteenth-note-based rhythms in the snare and bass drum. As mentioned on page 11, these straight time-playing patterns tend to be found in rock, funk, progressive rock, and fusion. It is recommended that you count the given subdivisions of these examples as we did with the examples above.

2+3 Subdivisions

More 2+3 Subdivisions

♩ = 90

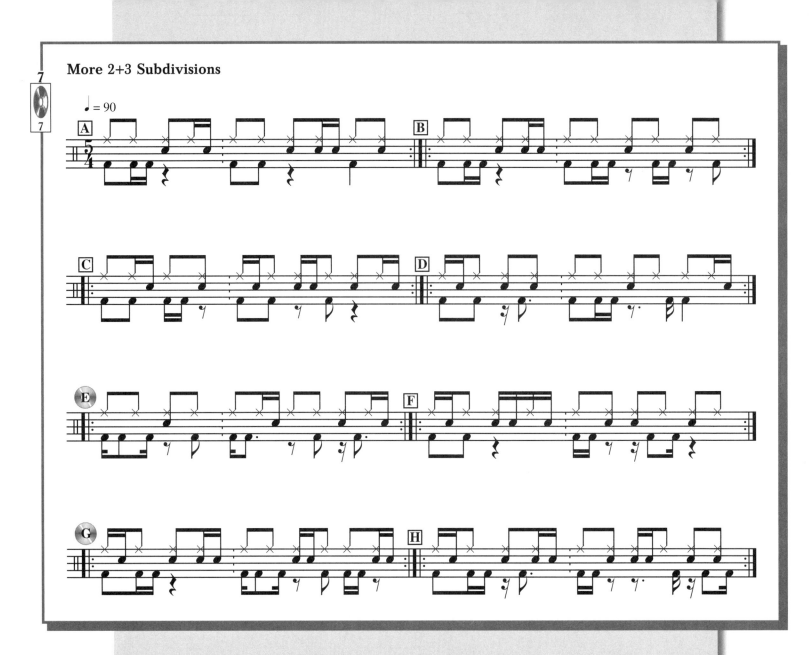

Now, let's try some 3+2 subdivisions. Remember to count the rhythms until they feel comfortable to you.

3+2 Subdivisions

♩ = 110

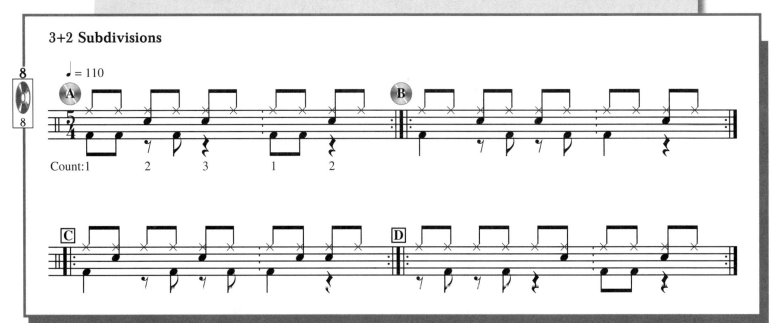

Count: 1   2   3   1   2

More 3+2 Subdivisions

HI-HAT AND CYMBAL VARIATIONS

Even though all of the straight eighth and sixteenth note examples are written with a constant eighth-note cymbal *ostinato* (repeated rhythmic pattern), this is only one of many possibilities. Once you have learned the patterns as written, practice applying alternate cymbal ostinatos to increase your time-playing vocabulary and give yourself even more musical options. Below are some other cymbal patterns that can be repeated over the bass and snare patterns found in the written examples. You should practice playing them on both the hi-hat and ride cymbal.

Here are some examples with a quarter-note cymbal ostinato.

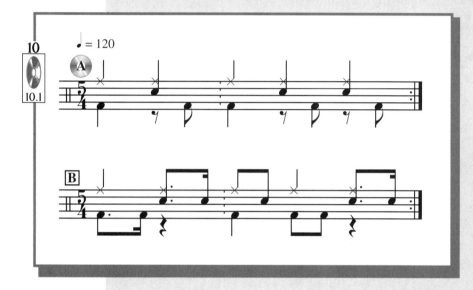

Below are a couple of examples using a sixteenth-note cymbal ostinato.

Following are some more cymbal ostinatos based on a quarter-note pulse. Feel free to apply the time-playing patterns from above to each ostinato pattern, or come up with your own time-playing patterns to create even more variations.

Another variation is to apply a swing feel to the straight examples we've been playing. This gives us a shuffle feel, which is common in blues music as well as rock, pop, and country styles.

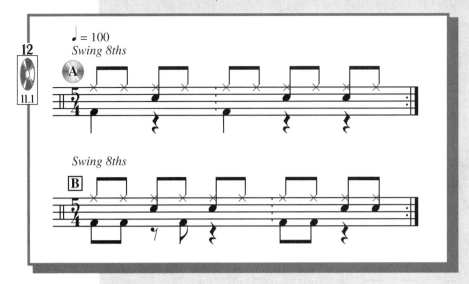

You can apply swing sixteenth notes to the sixteenth-note-based examples for a hip hop/swing funk feel.

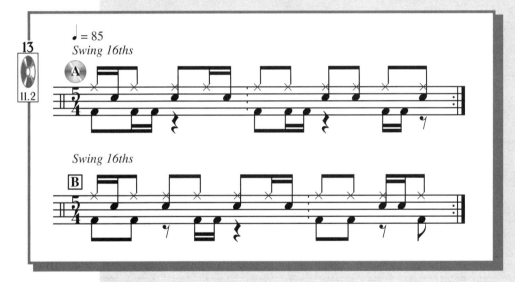

For even more variations, orchestrate the written snare drum patterns around the set.

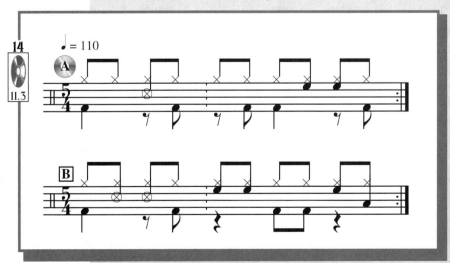

JAZZ IN $\frac{5}{4}$

Next are some examples of jazz time-playing/comping patterns in $\frac{5}{4}$ time. If you skipped Chapter Three, read the text on page 13 for the definition of comping and an explanation of how to approach the jazz exercises.

We will start with a simple time-playing pattern in $\frac{5}{4}$ with a 2+3 subdivision.

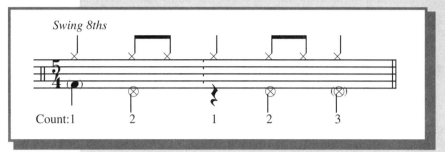

Now, let's try some comping ideas with the 2+3 subdivision.

2+3 Subdivisions

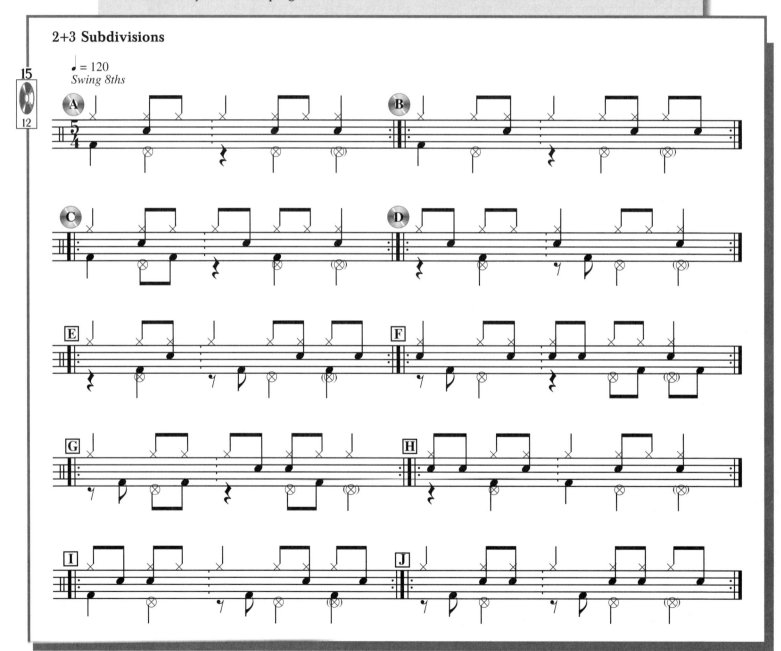

More 2+3 Subdivisions

After you become comfortable playing each individual exercise, mix and match them to create two-bar phrases. In an actual jazz performance, you will not be repeating one-bar phrases over and over. Creating longer phrases will help simulate the ever-changing rhythms that occur during the course of a jazz performance. Below is an example of a two-bar phrase in $\frac{5}{4}$.

After you get used to this, string together four one-bar examples to create four-bar phrases.

Next up are examples with a 3+2 subdivision of the bar. Remember, there is no rule that says the examples in this book are the only way to play jazz in $\frac{5}{4}$. Once you become comfortable with these exercises, experiment with your own ride cymbal and stepped hi-hat variations. And don't forget to play two- and four-bar phrases using different combinations of these examples.

3+2 Subdivisions

PLAYING IN $\frac{5}{8}$

This is where we really start getting into the concepts of pulse, subdivisions, and note groupings, particularly the idea of twos and threes. Although a measure of $\frac{5}{4}$ tends to subdivide into a group of two and a group of three, there is a constant quarter-note pulse throughout each measure. $\frac{5}{8}$, however, contains two different pulses: a quarter-note pulse and a dotted quarter-note pulse. In other words, each measure of $\frac{5}{8}$ subdivides into a group of two eighth notes and a group of three eighth notes. The group of two can be counted as "1, 2" and the group of three can be counted as "1, 2, 3." Sometimes these are thought of as a long pulse (dotted quarter note) and a short pulse (quarter note).

ROCK AND FUNK IN $\frac{5}{8}$

Following are examples of time-playing patterns in $\frac{5}{8}$, incorporating variations of straight eighth and sixteenth note rhythms in the snare and bass drum. These can be applied to rock, funk, progressive rock, and fusion styles.

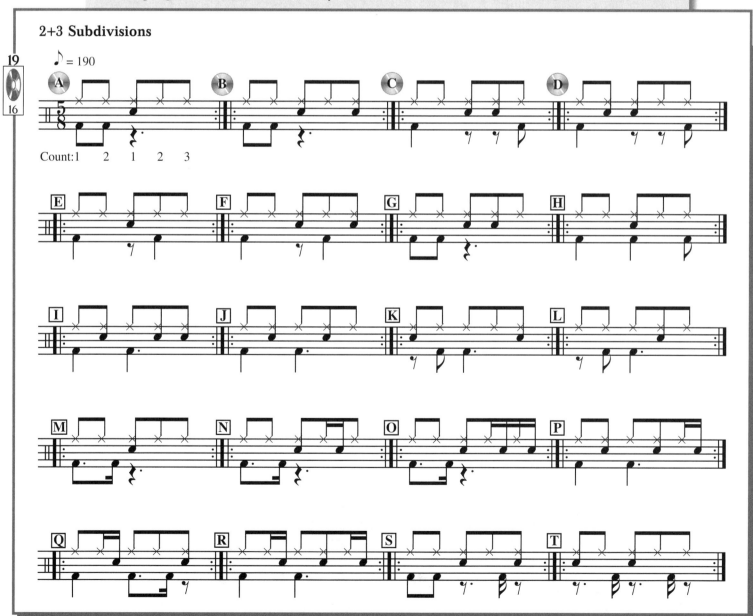

More 2+3 Subdivisions

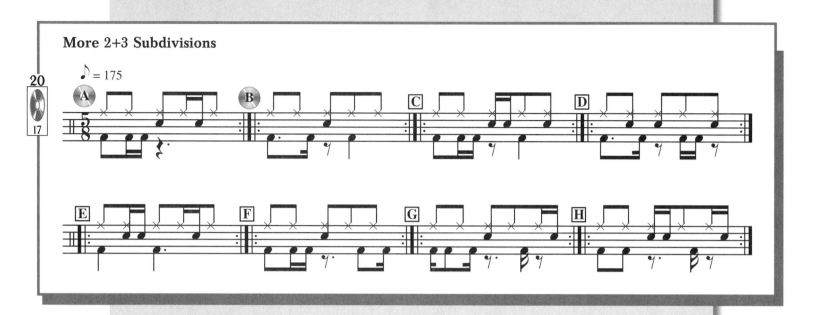

Now, let's try some rhythms with a subdivision of 3+2.

3+2 Subdivisions

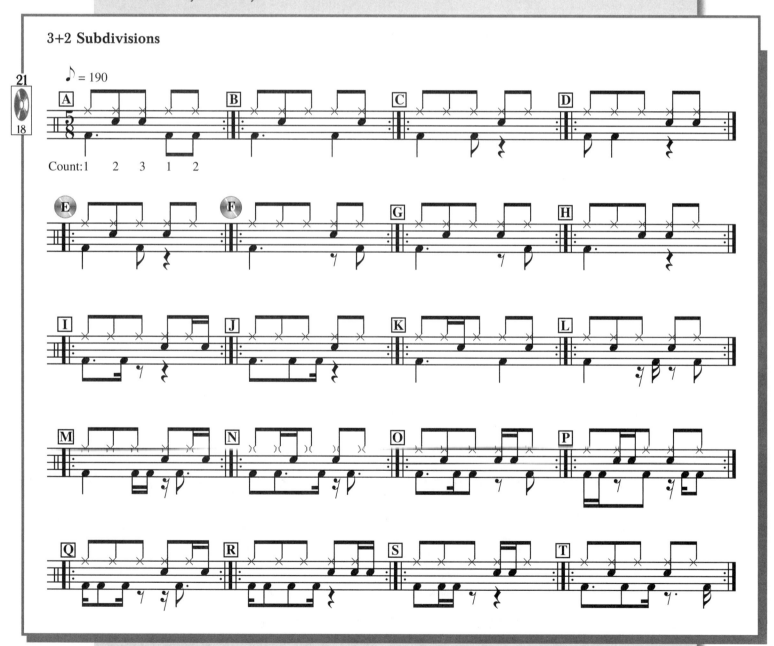

PLAYING IN $\frac{5}{16}$

$\frac{5}{16}$ is essentially the same as $\frac{5}{8}$. You might see the $\frac{5}{16}$ time signature (or any "16" time signature) if the tempo is particularly fast, or if the music is in *mixed meter* (time signatures change throughout the composition). The basic pulse of $\frac{5}{16}$ is an eighth note and a dotted eighth note. It is counted the same way as $\frac{5}{8}$.

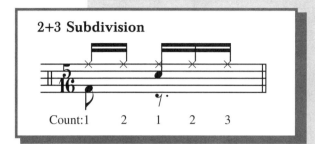

2+3 Subdivision

Count: 1 2 1 2 3

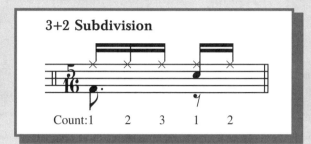

3+2 Subdivision

Count: 1 2 3 1 2

CYMBAL VARIATIONS

Time signatures such as $\frac{5}{8}$ and $\frac{5}{16}$ are often found in progressive rock and fusion. You can also hear time signatures such as $\frac{5}{8}$, $\frac{7}{8}$, $\frac{9}{8}$, and $\frac{11}{8}$ (the last few are coming up in the next two chapters) in Balkan folk and contemporary music. The style known as "Bulgarian wedding music" is full of odd time signatures. There are no traditional drum "beats" in this style. The drummers and percussionists tend to play off of the melody in whatever subdivision is being used at the time (2+3, for instance). There is often quite a bit of improvisation in this music. The cymbal patterns tend to be simplified (or "broken up") as opposed to steady eighth notes. Below are a couple of alternate cymbal patterns (examples A–D use one pattern and E–H use the other).

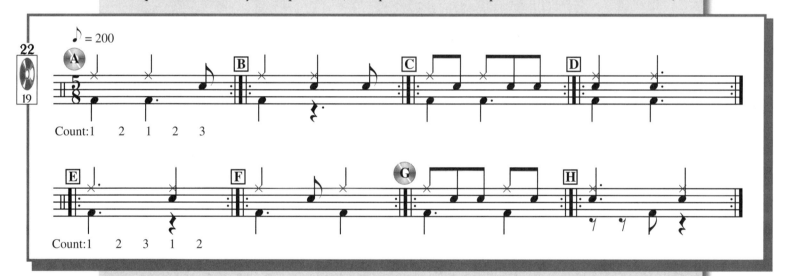

Here are two more variations.

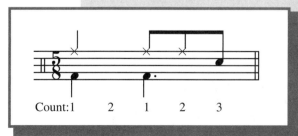

Count: 1 2 1 2 3

Count: 1 2 3 1 2

CHAPTER FIVE
TIME PLAYING IN SEVEN

PLAYING IN $\frac{7}{4}$

The basic concept of playing in seven is the same as playing in five. The measures subdivide into groups of two and three. If you can play in four (two groups of two equals four) and you can play in three, you can play in seven. The higher the top number of an odd time signature, the more possible ways there are to subdivide the bar. The most common subdivision for playing in seven is 2+2+3 (which can also be thought of as 4+3).

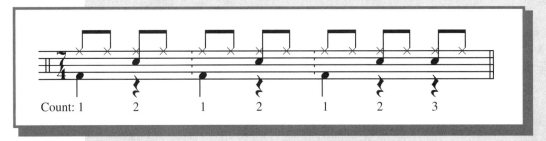

Another possible subdivision is 3+2+2 (or 3+4).

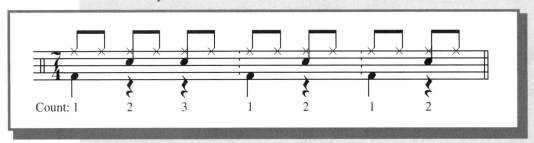

And finally, we have 2+3+2.

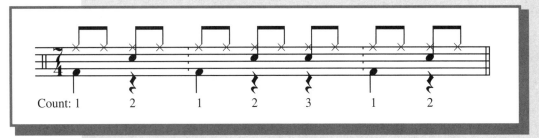

The groupings of two and three are not always as clear cut as the examples above and can sometimes be interpreted in more than one way based on the placement of the snare and bass drum. In this book, the examples are separated by the most strongly suggested subdivision of the bar. When applying these types of patterns to performance situations, listen to the melody and chord changes to help you figure out the appropriate subdivision.

ROCK AND FUNK IN $\frac{7}{4}$

Following are examples of straight-eighth and sixteenth-note patterns that are commonly found in rock, pop, funk, progressive rock, and fusion. When learning these patterns, count the subdivisions (for example: "1, 2, 1, 2, 1, 2, 3"). This will help you to get comfortable with the feel of the different subdivisions.

2+2+3 Subdivisions (4+3)

3+2+2 Subdivisions

2+3+2 Subdivisions

Below are a couple of examples with a quarter-note cymbal ostinato.

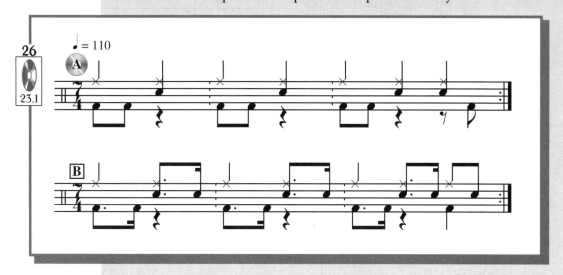

Here, we have a sixteenth-note cymbal ostinato.

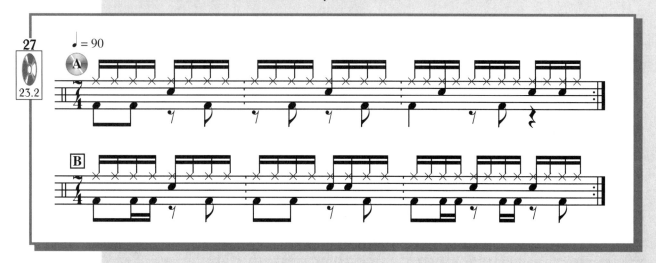

Below are more variations based on a quarter-note pulse.

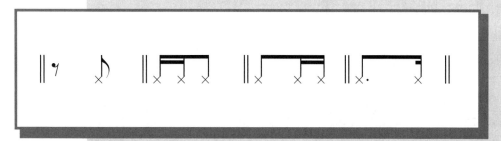

Now, try applying a swing feel to the $\frac{7}{4}$ examples we've been playing. This gives us a shuffle feel, which is common in blues music, as well as rock, pop, and country styles.

You can apply swing sixteenth notes for a hip hop/swing funk feel.

For even more variations on time playing, take the written snare drum patterns and orchestrate them around the set.

JAZZ IN $\frac{7}{4}$

Next are some examples of jazz time-playing/comping patterns in $\frac{7}{4}$ time. They should be practiced in the same manner as the $\frac{3}{4}$ and $\frac{5}{4}$ jazz examples in the previous two chapters.

We will start with a simple time-playing pattern in $\frac{7}{4}$ with a 2+2+3 subdivision.

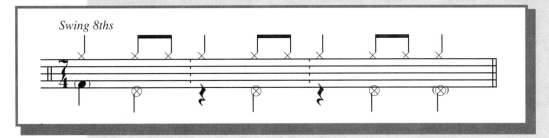

Now, let's try some comping ideas.

2+2+3 Subdivisions

More 2+2+3 Subdivisions

3+2+2 Subdivisions

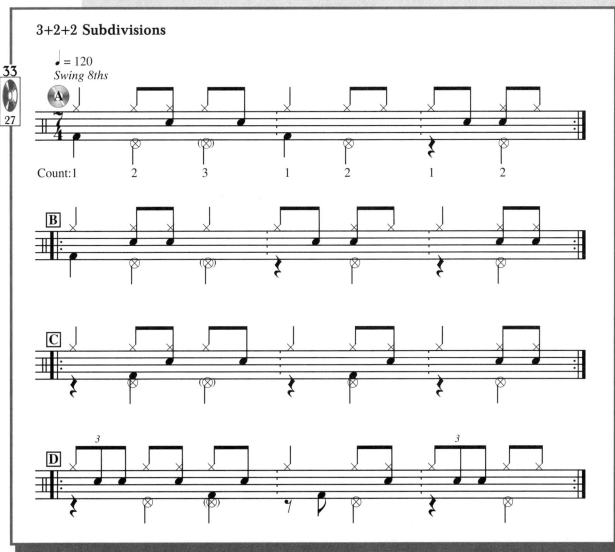

More 3+2+2 Subdivisions

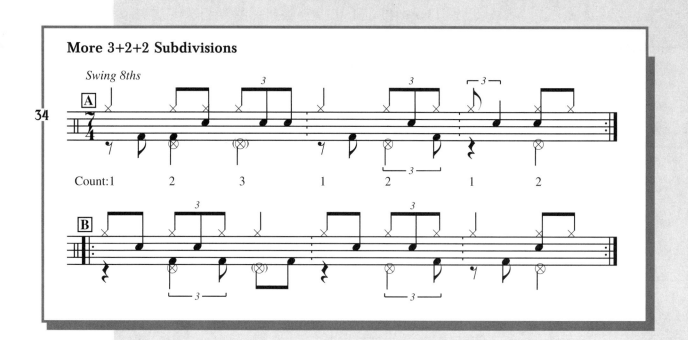

2+3+2 Subdivisions

PLAYING IN $\frac{7}{8}$

$\frac{7}{8}$ can be broken down into groups of two and three eighth notes or short (quarter note) and long (dotted quarter note) pulses just like $\frac{5}{8}$. When the top number of the time signature gets larger, the number of possible subdivisions of the bar also increases. In $\frac{7}{8}$, the bar can be subdivided into 2+2+3 (short, short, long), 3+2+2 (long, short, short), or 2+3+2 (short, long, short).

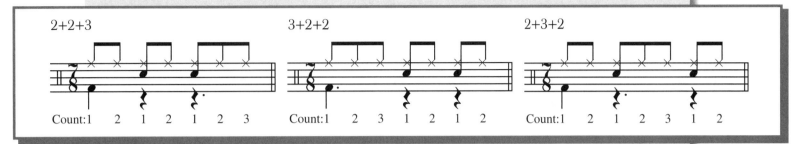

ROCK AND FUNK IN $\frac{7}{8}$

Following are some grooves in $\frac{7}{8}$. They can all be applied in rock, funk, progressive rock, and fusion settings.

2+2+3 Subdivisions

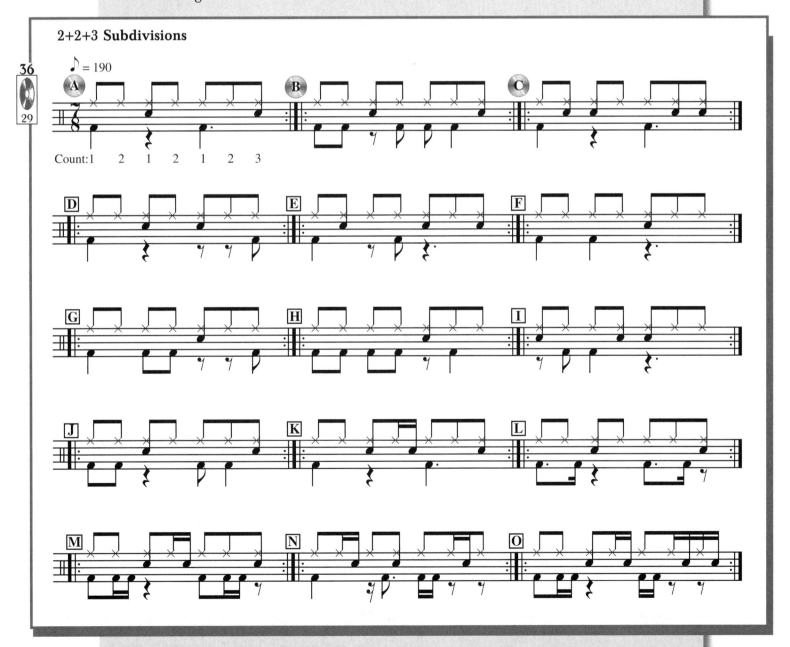

More 2+2+3 Subdivisions

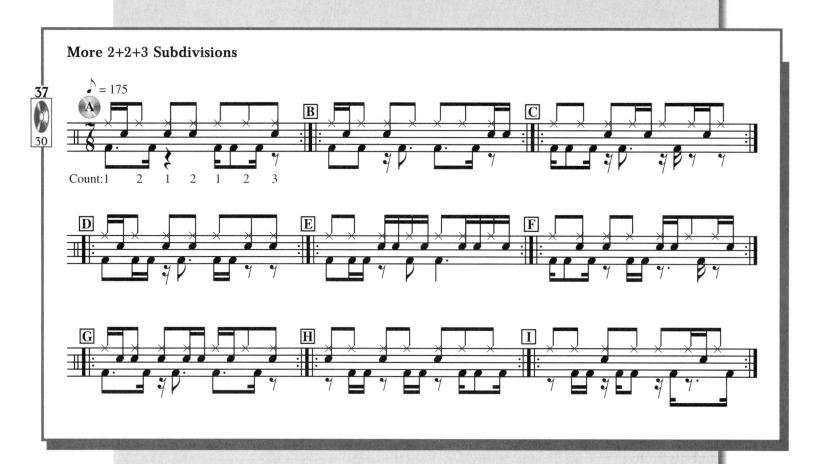

3+2+2 Subdivisions

More 3+2+2 Subdivisions

2+3+2 Subdivisions

PLAYING IN $\frac{7}{16}$

You might see the $\frac{7}{16}$ time signature (or any "16" time signature) if the tempo is particularly fast, or if the music is in mixed meter. The basic pulse of $\frac{7}{16}$ consists of some combination of two eighth notes and a dotted eighth note. It is counted the same way as $\frac{7}{8}$.

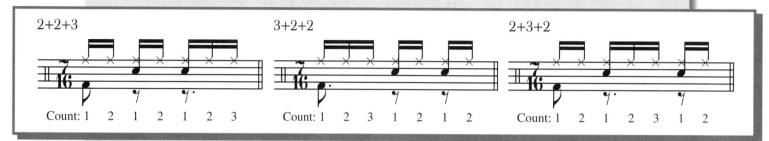

CYMBAL VARIATIONS

Time signatures such as $\frac{7}{8}$ and $\frac{7}{16}$ are often found in progressive rock and fusion music, as well as Balkan music, and some eastern European music and Middle Eastern music. As mentioned on page 27, it is not uncommon for the cymbal patterns to be simplified, especially at fast tempos. Following are some examples of alternate cymbal patterns.

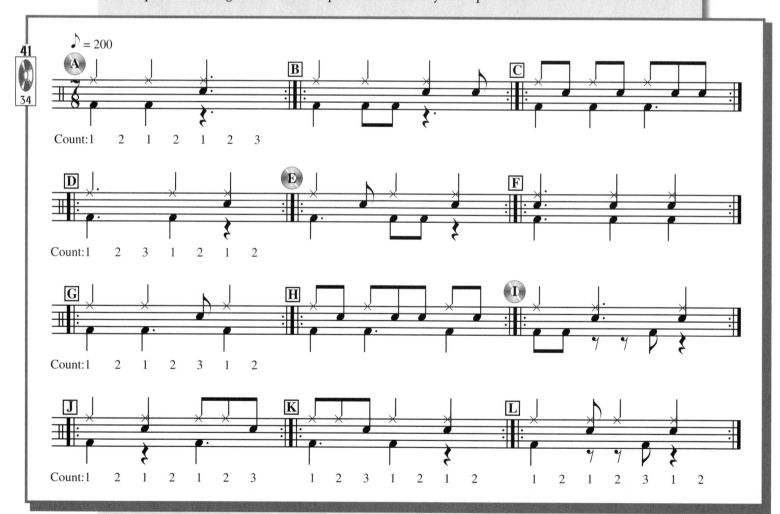

CHAPTER SIX
TIME PLAYING IN NINE, ELEVEN, AND OTHER ODD TIME SIGNATURES

The basic concept of feeling and playing odd time signatures larger than three is the same no matter what the specific time signature is. Subdivide the bars into smaller note groupings (twos and threes). If the pulse is a consistent quarter note (as with $\frac{5}{4}$ and $\frac{7}{4}$), then all you need to do is feel the groupings of two and three quarter notes. If the pulse is a mixture of quarter notes and dotted quarter notes (such as in $\frac{5}{8}$ and $\frac{7}{8}$), you need to play off of those pulses (which are still groups of two and three, only with eighth notes instead of quarter notes). This basic concept applies to all the rest of the odd time signatures ($\frac{9}{4}$, $\frac{9}{8}$, $\frac{11}{4}$, $\frac{11}{8}$, $\frac{13}{4}$, $\frac{13}{8}$, etc.). One exception is a version of nine where the bar is subdivided into three groups of three (which gives us three dotted quarter-note pulses). Here is a measure in $\frac{9}{8}$.

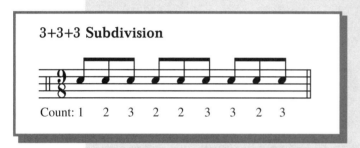

3+3+3 Subdivision

Count: 1 2 3 2 2 3 3 2 3

For the most part, the concept of twos and threes can be applied across the board. With this in mind, we will look at only a few musical examples in nine and eleven. Otherwise, this book would go on forever. If you can understand the basic concept of subdivisions, you can apply it to any odd time signature. As the time signatures become larger, the amount of possible subdivisions of the bar increases, but they can all be broken down into smaller, more manageable parts. The raw materials are the same. If you can play in $\frac{2}{4}$, $\frac{3}{4}$ and $\frac{4}{4}$, you can play in any "quarter note" time signature ($\frac{5}{4}$, $\frac{7}{4}$, $\frac{5}{4}$, $\frac{11}{4}$, etc.). The meter $\frac{9}{4}$ can be subdivided as 3+3+3, but it can also be thought of as 2+2+2+3, or some combination of $\frac{4}{4}$ and $\frac{5}{4}$.

ROCK AND FUNK IN $\frac{9}{4}$

Following are some time-playing patterns in $\frac{9}{4}$ that can be used in rock and funk settings.

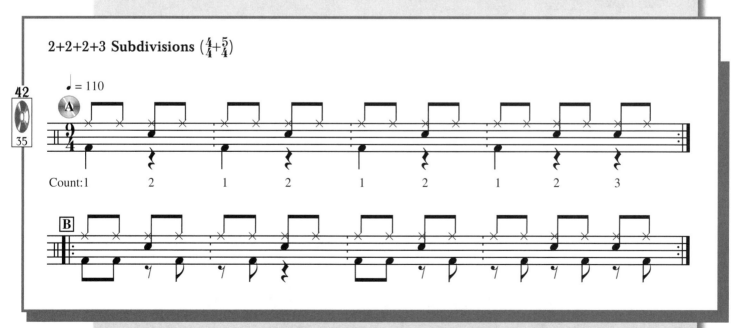

2+2+2+3 Subdivisions ($\frac{4}{4}+\frac{5}{4}$)

♩ = 110

Count: 1 2 1 2 1 2 1 2 3

Following are some more patterns in $\frac{9}{4}$ using other possible subdivisions.

3+2+2+2 Subdivision ($\frac{5}{4}$+$\frac{4}{4}$)

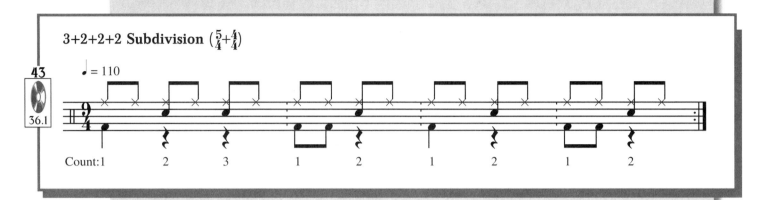

2+3+2+2 Subdivision ($\frac{5}{4}$+$\frac{4}{4}$)

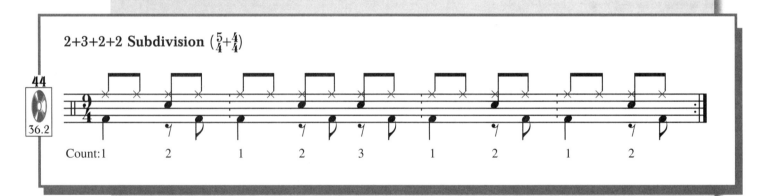

2+2+3+2 Subdivision ($\frac{4}{4}$+$\frac{5}{4}$)

JAZZ IN $\frac{9}{4}$

The same idea applies to jazz time playing in $\frac{9}{4}$. Below are some $\frac{9}{4}$ jazz examples with simple snare drum comping ideas.

2+2+2+3 Subdivision ($\frac{4}{4}+\frac{5}{4}$)

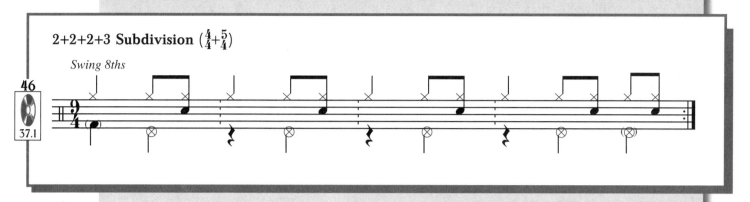

3+2+2+2 Subdivision ($\frac{5}{4}+\frac{4}{4}$)

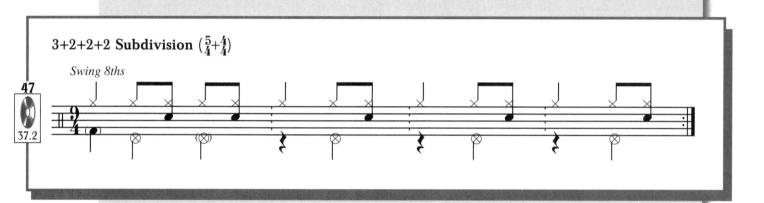

2+3+2+2 Subdivision ($\frac{5}{4}+\frac{4}{4}$)

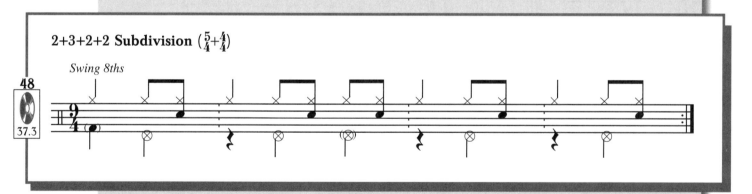

2+2+3+2 Subdivision ($\frac{4}{4}+\frac{5}{4}$)

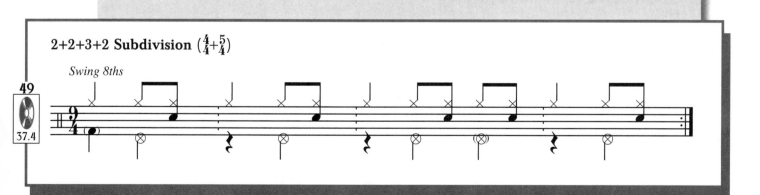

PLAYING IN $\frac{9}{8}$

The most common subdivision in $\frac{9}{8}$ time is 2+2+2+3. This subdivision can readily be found in Balkan music (especially Turkish, Greek, and Bulgarian). A jazz example using this subdivision is the tune "Blue Rondo à la Turk" by The Dave Brubeck Quartet. There is a section of the tune that switches between 2+2+2+3 (played for three bars) and 3+3+3 (played for one bar). Another section is in $\frac{4}{4}$. This is a great example of mixed meter and mixed subdivisions of odd times. The end result is an enjoyable and interesting piece of music. There is a lesson to be learned here. The use of odd time signatures, mixed time signatures, and mixed subdivisions of odd time signatures can (and should) be quite musical. These concepts should not be used as devices to sound clever. A beautiful piece of music in $\frac{4}{4}$ has more value than a poorly constructed piece of music in an odd time signature.

Below are some time playing examples in $\frac{9}{8}$.

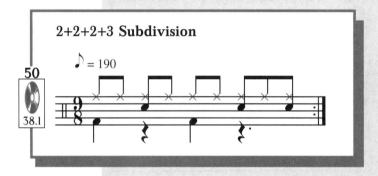

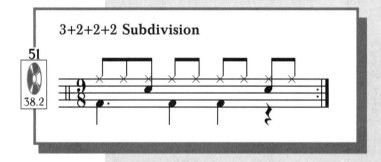

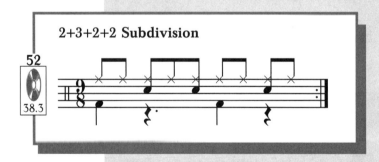

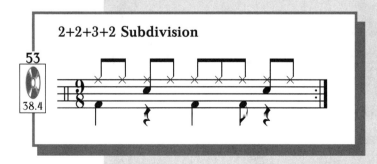

PLAYING IN $\frac{11}{4}$

Now, let's look at $\frac{11}{4}$. This time signature can be broken down into different subdivisions just like the other meters in this book.

Following are some examples of time-playing patterns in $\frac{11}{4}$. We'll look at three different subdivisions.

3+3+3+2 Subdivision

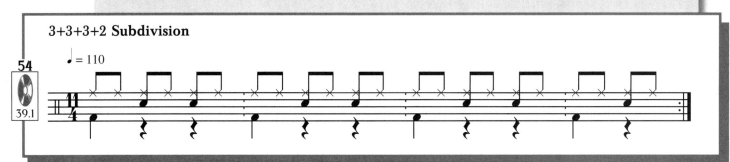

2+2+2+2+3 Subdivision ($\frac{4}{4}+\frac{7}{4}$)

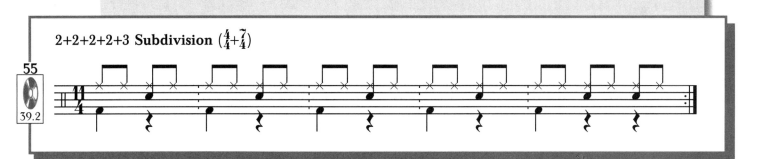

2+2+3+2+2 Subdivision ($\frac{7}{4}+\frac{4}{4}$)

JAZZ IN $\frac{11}{4}$

Here are a few $\frac{11}{4}$ jazz patterns with simple snare drum comping ideas.

3+3+3+2 Subdivision

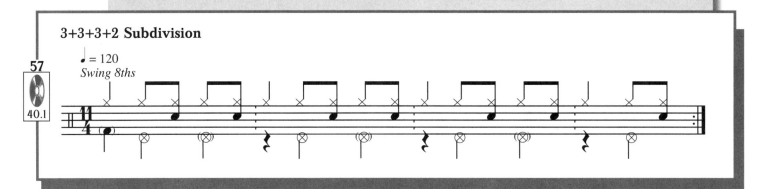

2+2+2+2+3 Subdivision ($\frac{4}{4}+\frac{7}{4}$)

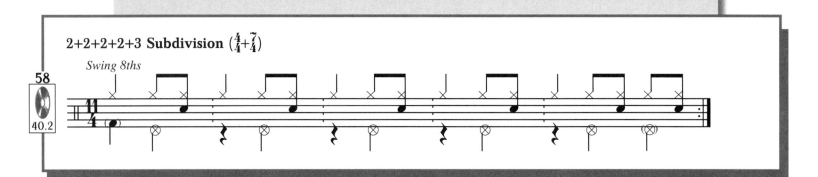

2+2+3+2+2 Subdivision ($\frac{7}{4}+\frac{4}{4}$)

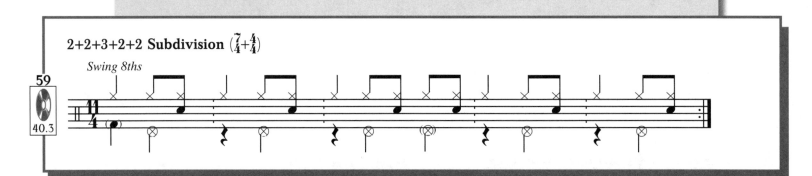

PLAYING IN $\frac{11}{8}$

Here are some examples in $\frac{11}{8}$. Remember, the subdivisions we used for $\frac{11}{4}$ also work in $\frac{11}{8}$.

3+3+3+2 Subdivision

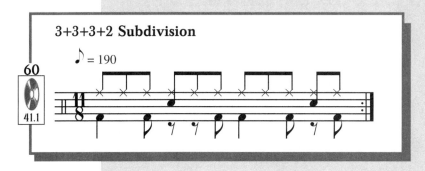

2+2+2+2+3 Subdivision

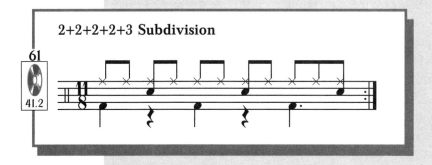

2+2+3+2+2 Subdivision

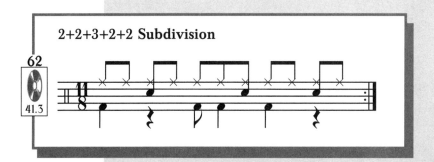

The 2+2+3+2+2 subdivision is often found in Bulgarian wedding music. Here is one way to play it at the fast tempos common in this style.

CHAPTER SEVEN
APPLYING ODD TIME SIGNATURES TO BRAZILIAN RHYTHMS

So far, we have been looking at odd time signatures as they might be found in styles such as rock, pop, punk, heavy metal, progressive rock, blues, jazz, jazz/rock fusion, and hip hop. Now, we're going to look at ways to adapt odd time signatures to musical styles that do not traditionally make use of them.

SAMBA

Let's start with the Brazilian rhythm called *samba*. Samba is often applied to jazz and fusion settings. It is a style that every working drummer should know. It is important to understand that samba has been around much longer than the drumset. There is not one "correct" way to play samba on the kit. If you are completely unfamiliar with this style, it is recommended that you familiarize yourself with the basic concepts, sound, and feel of this music. Listening to Brazilian musicians playing samba is invaluable. There are many compilations you can purchase, or borrow from your local public library. Notes on paper can only get you so far.

For those of you who are not familiar with this style, we will quickly go over a common drumset samba rhythm and then look at some odd time applications. It is important that this style be played with a light feeling. Do not lay into the drums and cymbals as you would in a rock or funk setting. Following is a common samba rhythm applied to the drumset.

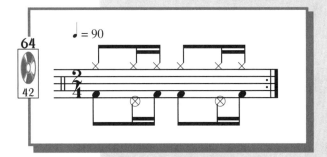

You should at least play the bass drum notes on beats 1 and 2. The bass drum upbeat (the last sixteenth note of each beat) and the stepped hi-hat can be left out. For a more authentic sound, slightly accent the bass drum on beat 2.

The hand that is not playing the cymbal is used to play rhythmic variations. (This is notated for cross-stick, but can also be played on the snare drum or orchestrated around the drumset.) These variations sometimes double the rhythm being played by another instrument such as the guitar or keyboard. They might also be used as comping ideas during a solo, or, to accentuate the melody of a composition.

Following is a two-bar phrase in $\frac{2}{4}$ with samba time playing and one of many possible cross-stick variations. This particular variation is a rhythm known as *partido alto*.

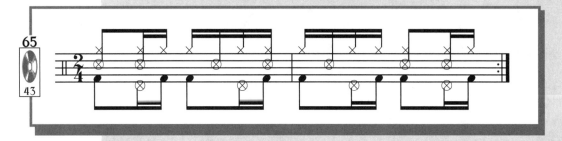

SAMBA IN $\frac{3}{4}$

Keep in mind that the following examples are odd time adaptations of the samba rhythm. Traditional samba patterns are not in odd time signatures. The exercises are intended to help you with applying the samba to *world fusion music* situations. (World fusion music is a blending of musical styles from around the world, as well as contemporary styles like rock and jazz.) As mentioned in previous chapters, use your ears and let the music determine what you play.

The cymbal and foot pattern for a $\frac{3}{4}$ samba is the same as the $\frac{2}{4}$ example.

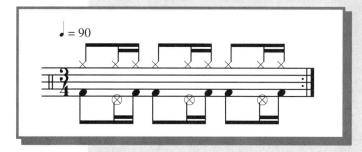

Here is an example of a two-bar phrase with some cross-stick patterns.

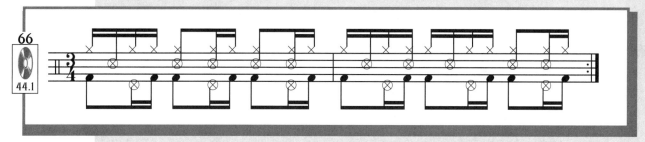

Another approach is to play both hands in unison (both hands playing the same rhythm at the same time).

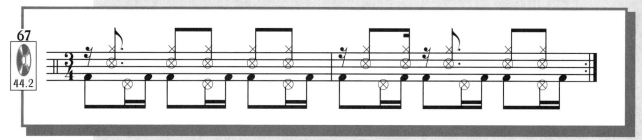

The following approach involves playing constant sixteenth notes on the snare with brushes. The cross-stick rhythms from the previous examples are played as accented sixteenth notes.

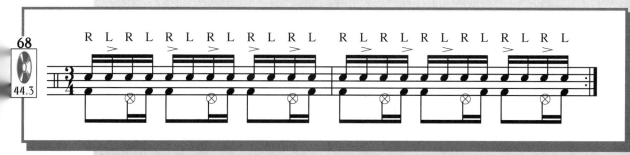

R = Right hand
L = Left hand

Following is another two-bar example using a different rhythm.

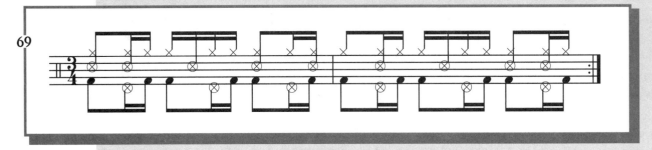

Here it is using unison hands.

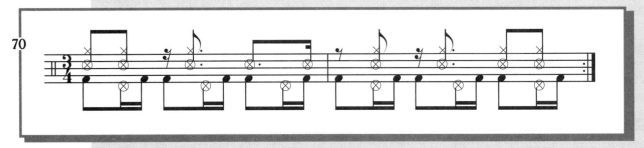

Here it is using brushes and accented sixteenth notes.

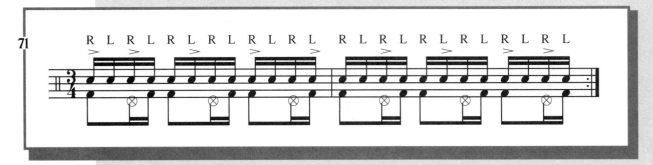

Now, it's time to move on to samba in five and seven. The following examples in $\frac{5}{4}$ and $\frac{7}{4}$ do not have a clear sense of being subdivided into twos and threes. They are simply in five or seven. If the composition you are playing is subdivided, the *harmonic rhythm* (placement of chord changes within the composition) and phrasing of the melody will clue you in to which subdivision is being used—use your ears! (The examples in $\frac{5}{8}$ and $\frac{7}{8}$ *will* have clear subdivisions.)

SAMBA IN $\frac{5}{4}$

Following is a one-bar example of samba applied to $\frac{5}{4}$.

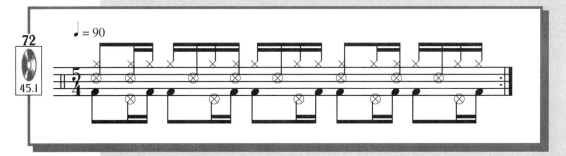

Here it is with unison hands.

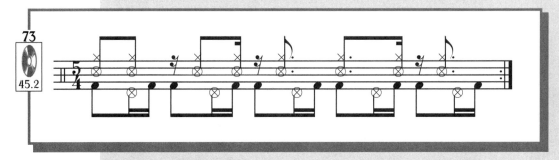

Here it is using brushes and accented sixteenth notes.

Here is another one-bar example of samba applied to $\frac{5}{4}$.

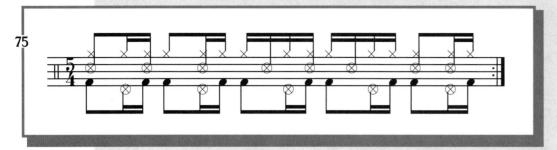

With unison hands:

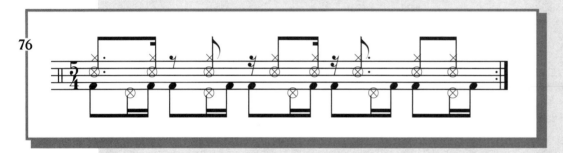

With brushes and accented sixteenth notes:

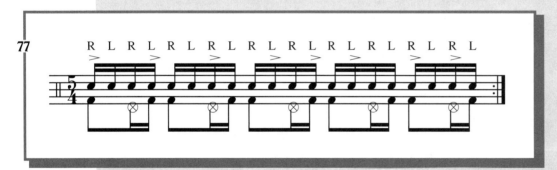

SAMBA IN $\frac{5}{8}$

Below is a cymbal and foot pattern that works well in a 2+3 subdivision of $\frac{5}{8}$.

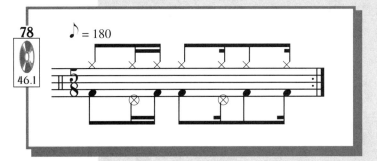

Here is a two-bar phrase with a cross-stick rhythm.

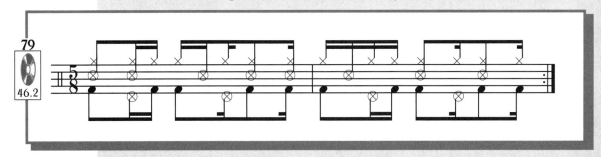

With unison hands:

With brushes and accented sixteenth notes:

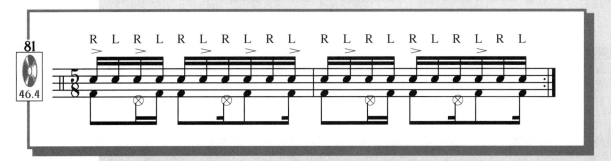

Now, let's take a look at a cymbal and foot pattern with a 3+2 subdivision of $\frac{5}{8}$.

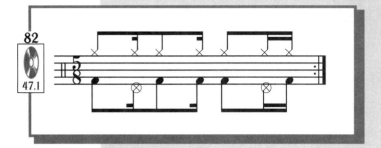

Here is a two-bar phrase with a cross-stick rhythm.

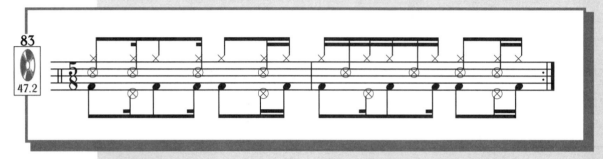

With unison hands:

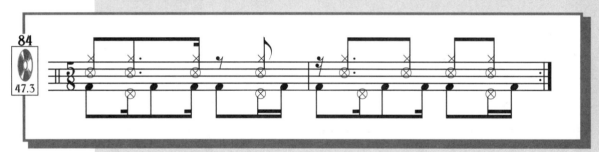

With brushes and accented sixteenth notes:

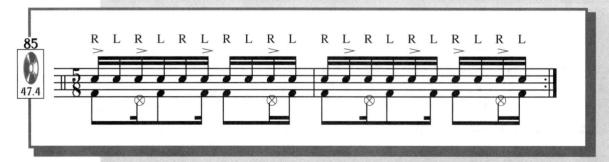

SAMBA IN $\frac{7}{4}$

Now, let's move on to a one-bar example of samba in $\frac{7}{4}$.

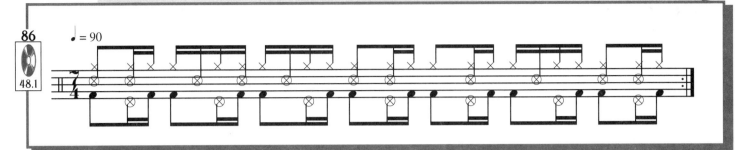

With unison hands:

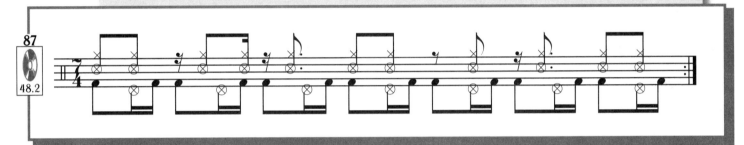

With brushes and accented sixteenth notes:

Here's one more samba example in $\frac{7}{4}$.

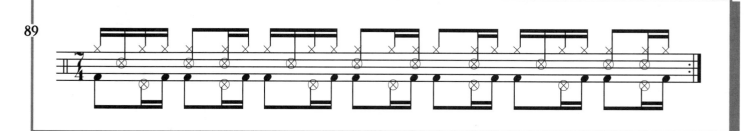

With unison hands:

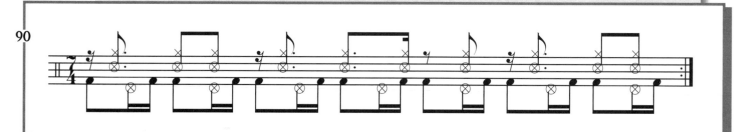

With brushes and accented sixteenth notes:

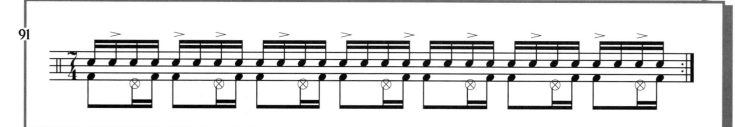

SAMBA IN $\frac{7}{8}$

The following cymbal and foot pattern works well for samba with a 2+2+3 subdivision of $\frac{7}{8}$.

92
49.1

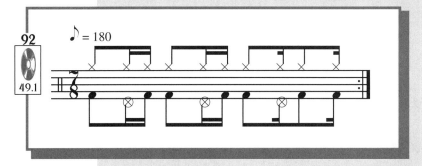

Here is a one-bar example with a cross-stick variation.

93
49.2

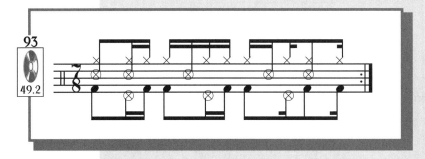

With unison hands:

94
49.3

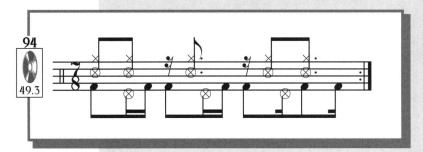

With brushes and accented sixteenth notes:

95
49.4

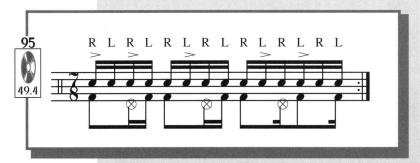

Below is a cymbal and foot pattern that works well for samba with a 3+2+2 subdivision of $\frac{7}{8}$.

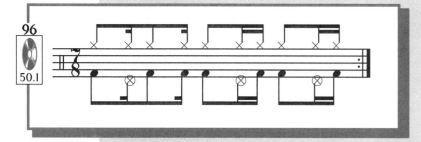

Here is a one-bar example with a cross-stick variation.

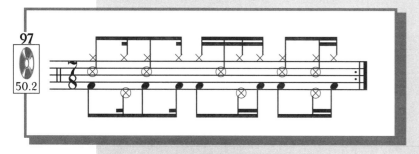

With unison hands:

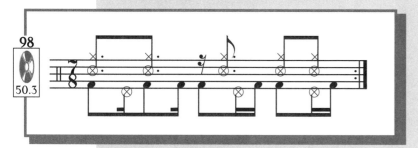

With brushes and accented sixteenth notes:

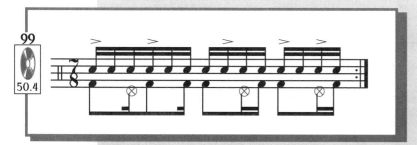

SAMBA IN $\frac{9}{8}$

Following are some possibilities for playing samba in $\frac{9}{8}$.

2+2+2+3 Subdivision

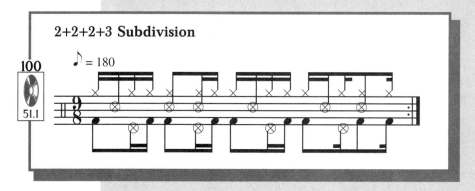

3+2+2+2 Subdivision

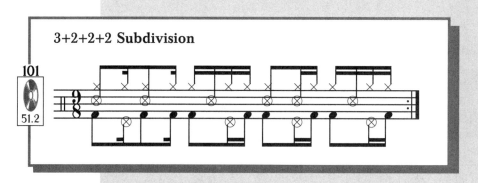

2+3+2+2 Subdivision

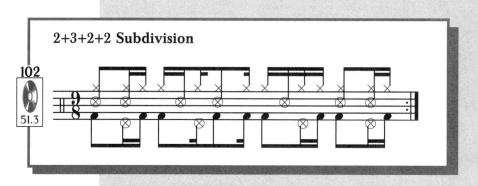

2+2+3+2 Subdivision

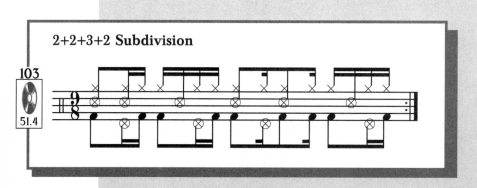

SAMBA IN $\frac{11}{8}$

Following are two different subdivisions of $\frac{11}{8}$ with a samba application.

104 **2+2+2+2+3 Subdivision**

52.1

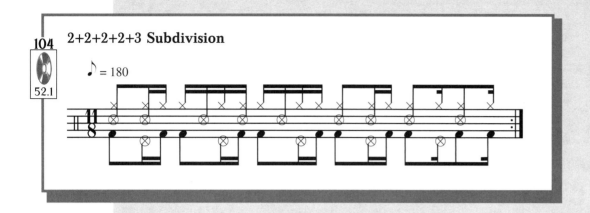

105 **2+2+3+2+2 Subdivision**

52.2

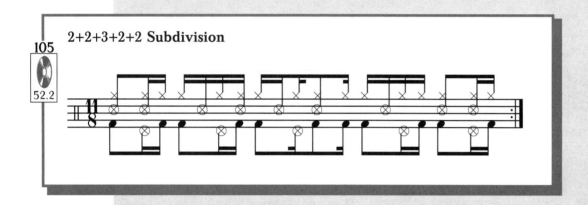

Now, let's move on to some odd time *bossa nova* applications.

BOSSA NOVA

Bossa nova is a Brazilian style that gained widespread popularity in the early 1960s. This style combines a "slowed down" samba feel with jazz harmony. Drummers are often called upon to play bossa nova in jazz and pop situations, so it is a good style to know. In bossa nova time playing, the foot pattern is essentially a *half time* version of the samba foot pattern. ("Half time" just means that the note values last twice as long.) As with the samba, you can choose not to play the bass drum upbeats and stepped hi-hat. A common drumset application of bossa nova has the cymbal hand playing straight eighth notes. Bossa nova should be played with a light touch. Do not lay into the cymbal and bass drum as you would in a rock or funk setting. For a lighter sound, you can play the cymbal part with a brush on the snare drum. Following is a common bossa nova rhythm.

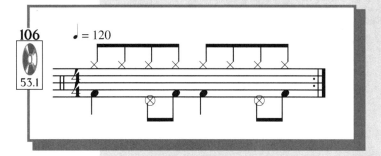

The opposite hand plays rhythmic variations (usually with the cross-stick). These ideas are often played in two-bar phrases. Following is a commonly played bossa nova cross-stick variation.

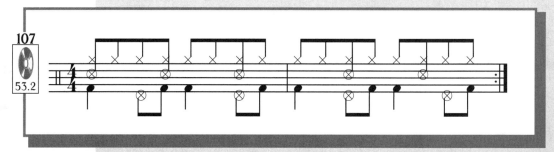

The following variation involves the cymbal hand playing an eighth-note rhythm in a side-to-side sweeping motion with a brush. You can play the brush part on the snare or another coated/textured drumhead. This creates a sound similar to a shaker.

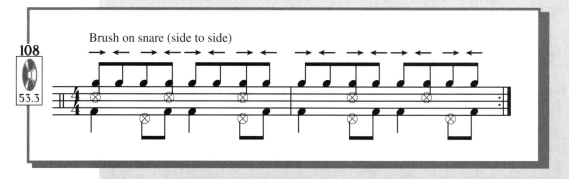

As mentioned in the samba section, you need to listen to music in this style to really get it. Working on exercises alone will not help you completely understand the feel and application of these rhythms.

BOSSA NOVA IN $\frac{5}{4}$

One way to get a $\frac{5}{4}$ bossa nova pattern is to take a $\frac{5}{8}$ samba pattern and "stretch it out" to half time, then play even eighth notes on the cymbal. Here is an example based on the 2+3 subdivision of five.

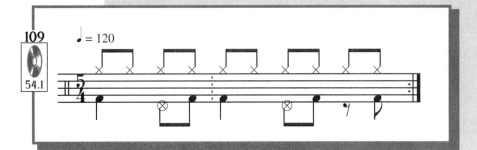

Now, we have a two-bar phrase with an added cross-stick variation.

Below, the subdivision is reversed (3+2 this time).

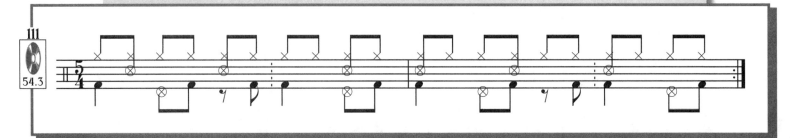

BOSSA NOVA IN $\frac{7}{4}$

Here is an example of bossa nova in $\frac{7}{4}$ with a 2+2+3 subdivision.

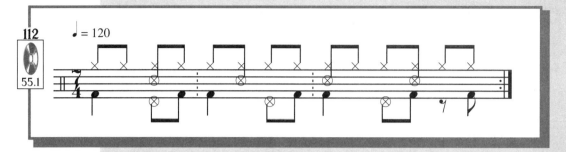

Here's one with a 3+2+2 subdivision.

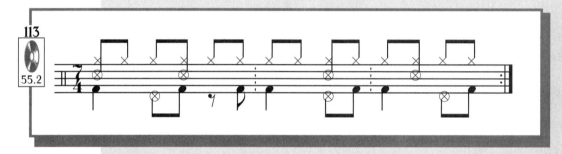

Here's another with a 2+3+2 subdivision.

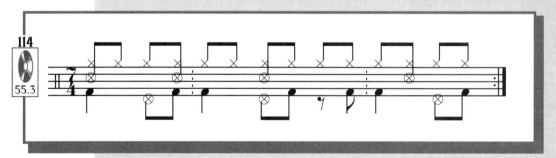

CHAPTER EIGHT
APPLYING ODD TIME SIGNATURES TO AFRO-CUBAN RHYTHMS

Afro-Cuban rhythms can also be adapted to odd time signatures. As with the Brazilian rhythms in the previous chapter, traditional Afro-Cuban rhythms do not make use of odd time signatures. The examples in this chapter show you various ways to apply these rhythms in world fusion music situations. If you are not already familiar with traditional Afro-Cuban rhythms, you owe it to yourself to investigate them. Every working drummer needs to have at least some knowledge of these styles. Be sure to listen to the music. Do not just look at patterns in a book.

The underlying rhythm on which Afro-Cuban music is based is the *clave.* If you are interested in playing traditional Afro-Cuban music, it is crucial that you become familiar with this concept. However, since we are taking these rhythms out of their traditional context, we will not be focusing on the clave.

MAMBO

A popular Afro-Cuban rhythm that has found its way into jazz, rock, and pop is the *mambo.* This rhythm, which is traditionally played on several percussion instruments (timbales, conga, cowbell, etc.), can be adapted to the drumset. The cowbell rhythm can be played with the right hand (usually on a cowbell or ride cymbal bell), and the conga slap and "open tone" sounds can be played with the left hand. (The slap sound can be played as a cross-stick, and the open tones can be played on the small tom.)

Following is the mambo bell pattern.

Here it is with the conga part added.

Now, here it is with the bass drum added. This bass drum rhythm is known as *tumbao,* which is an ostinato (repeated rhythmic pattern) performed by the bass player.

MAMBO IN $\frac{7}{4}$

By leaving out the last beat of the second bar we get the following $\frac{7}{4}$ mambo variation.

Here is a variation with two open tones played on the high tom on the last beat of the bar.

Another variation would be to start on the second bar of the two-bar phrase in $\frac{4}{4}$ and leave out the last beat of the first bar. This variation might be a bit tricky at first since it starts on an upbeat. If necessary, you can play a bass drum note on beat 1 to help anchor the time.

Here is a variation with some added open tones.

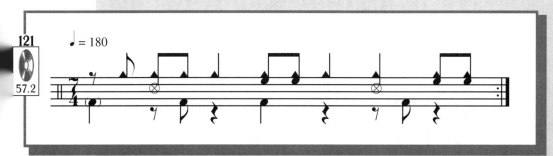

The ride hand can also play a rhythm known as *cascara*. The word cascara means "shell." This rhythm tends to be played by the timbale player on the shell of the drum during softer sections of a tune. You can play this pattern on the shell or rim of the snare or low tom, on a cowbell, on the ride cymbal, or on the ride cymbal bell. A common drumset application of cascara is to play it during softer sections of a composition (on the shell, rim, or ride cymbal). When it is time to increase the energy, you can switch to playing the mambo bell pattern on a cowbell or the ride cymbal bell.

Below is an example of the bass drum and snare hand pattern from the mambo example on page 64, with the ride hand playing cascara.

Here is a $\frac{7}{4}$ variation with open tones on the high tom played on beat 7.

Here is another $\frac{7}{4}$ variation. This time, we'll start with the second bar and play open tones on beat 7.

SONGO IN $\frac{7}{4}$

Another Afro-Cuban rhythm that adapts well to $\frac{7}{4}$ is *songo*. This is a relatively recent rhythm that was developed on the drumset.

The standard songo pattern can be notated as a two-bar phrase in $\frac{4}{4}$.

Now, let's adapt the songo rhythm to $\frac{7}{4}$ by dropping the last beat of the second bar to get a 2+2+3 subdivision.

Starting on the second bar of the original phrase and dropping the last beat of bar 1, we get another 2+2+3 subdivision.

By dropping the third beat of the first bar, we get this 3+2+2 variation.

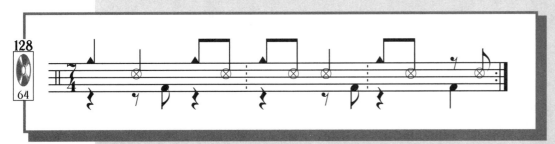

Starting on the second bar of the original phrase and dropping the last beat of bar 1, we get yet another 3+2+2 subdivision.

In the next example, you can play the cross-stick pattern on the snare drum or alternate between the snare and the toms to create more variations.

SONGO IN $\frac{5}{4}$

By adding a beat to each bar of the traditional $\frac{4}{4}$ songo, you get some interesting $\frac{5}{4}$ variations. In the following example, we get a 2+3 subdivision.

Now, let's start on the second bar of the example above.

In the next example, an extra beat is added after beat 2 of each $\frac{4}{4}$ bar to create a $\frac{5}{4}$ variation with a 3+2 subdivision.

Let's start on the second bar of the example above.

SONGO IN $\frac{9}{4}$

You can come up with $\frac{9}{4}$ songo variations by combining a bar of the standard $\frac{4}{4}$ songo and a bar of $\frac{5}{4}$ songo. Following are examples of $\frac{9}{4}$ songo variations in four different subdivisions.

2+2+2+3 Subdivision

135
71

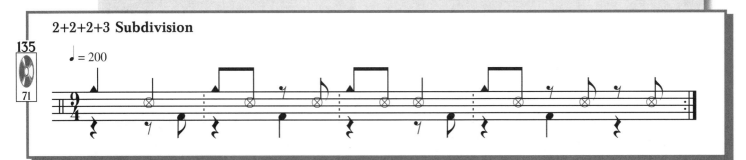

3+2+2+2 Subdivision

136
72

2+3+2+2 Subdivision

137
73

2+2+3+2 Subdivision

138
74

Try switching bars around to come up with other variations. Experiment and have fun!

CHAPTER NINE
PLAYING FILLS IN ODD TIME SIGNATURES

More often than not, a drum *fill* is used to announce an "event" in a musical arrangement. Examples of an event would be a transition from one section of a composition to another, or going back to the beginning of a repeated section of a composition. Drum fills can also be used for intros (also called *pickups*).

In this chapter, you will be given sample four-bar phrases, in different time signatures, that will be followed by a series of fills. The first three bars of the four-bar phrase will have a time-playing pattern. The fourth bar will have space for fills of varying lengths (one beat, two beats, etc.). Take each fill and place it in the fourth bar of each phrase. The fills will be based on eighth- and sixteenth-note subdivisions of quarter notes, triplet subdivisions of quarter notes, and eighth- and sixteenth-note subdivisions of dotted quarter notes. Playing four-bar phrases will help put the fill ideas into a context similar to an actual performance situation. Make sure to count each bar. Knowing where you are in the phrase at all times is a must. Counting in the practice room will help you get to a point where you can feel phrases go by in a performance situation. Repeat each four-bar phrase so you get to practice transitioning from time playing to fill playing and back again. Smooth transitions are crucial in an ensemble performance. There should be no hesitation when moving from one musical idea to another.

It is important to play off of the melody (and chord changes) of the composition and the subdivision of the bar and rely less on counting, particularly when soloing or playing longer fills. This will help to keep you from getting lost. More importantly, it will help you to play ideas that are more strongly connected to the music instead of just stringing random "drum stuff" together. Once the written examples become comfortable, you are encouraged to combine and orchestrate different one-beat cells to create your own fill and solo ideas.

Keep in mind that odd time fills and solos should groove and feel just as good as they would in $\frac{4}{4}$.

Note: The sticking patterns in the following examples are written for right-handed players and are merely suggestions. Feel free to experiment with your own sticking patterns.

Here is how it works:

Four-bar phrase example in $\frac{5}{4}$:

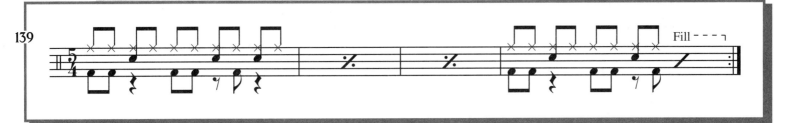

Fill:

Now, put the fill into the four-bar phrase:

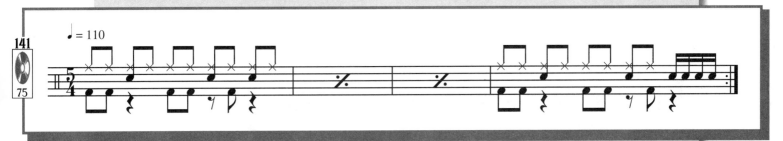

It's that simple!

Once you have learned the written examples, try using other time-playing patterns with the fills. You can use examples from the book, but are encouraged to come up with your own variations. You can also take the rhythmic cells from pages 9 and 10 and orchestrate them around the drumset to create your own fill variations.

FILLS IN A STRAIGHT TIME QUARTER-NOTE PULSE

The first group of fill ideas will be based on straight eighth- and sixteenth-note subdivisions of a quarter-note pulse. These types of fills are commonly found in styles such as rock, pop, funk, and contemporary country music. On the CD, you will hear only the last measure with the included fill. However, you should play the full four measures and repeat them several times to get the feel of each fill and how it fits in with the beat. In addition, the four-bar phrases will be in $\frac{5}{4}$ and $\frac{7}{4}$, but on the CD, only the phrases in $\frac{7}{4}$ will be used.

Four-Bar Phrases

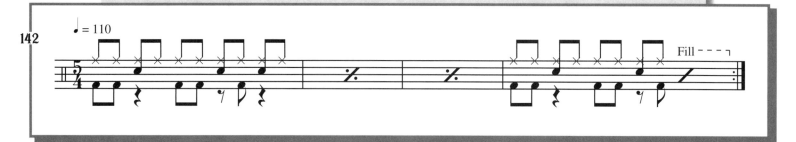

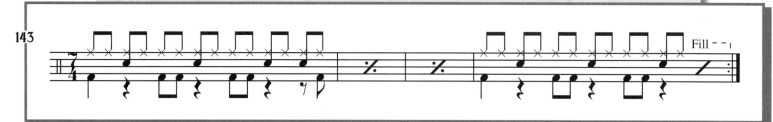

One-Beat Fills

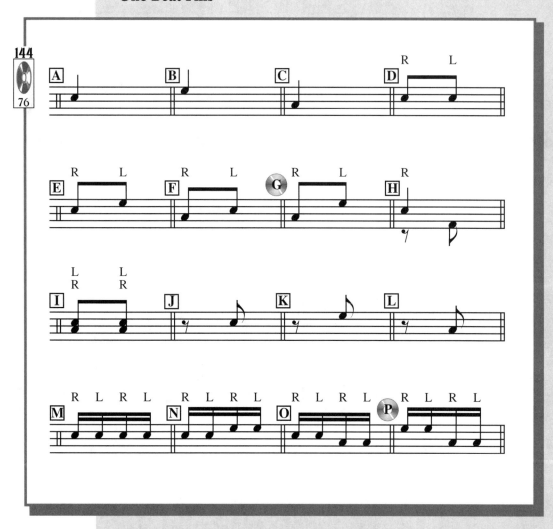

More One-Beat Fills

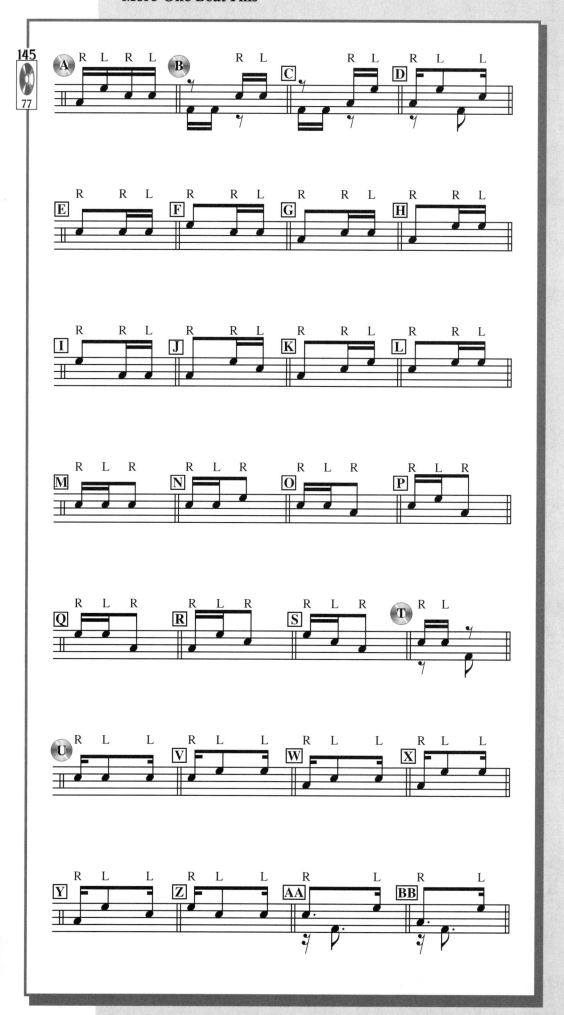

Four-Bar Phrases

Two-Beat Fills

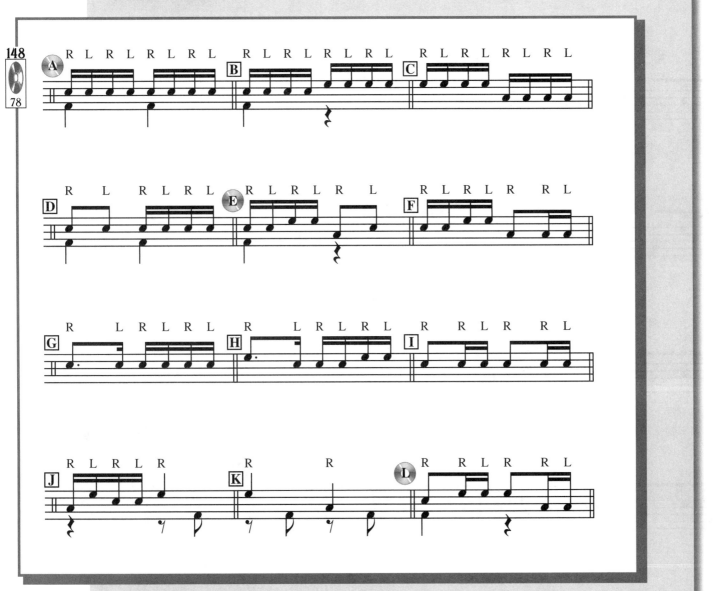

Four-Bar Phrases

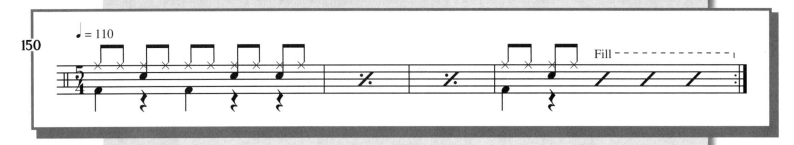

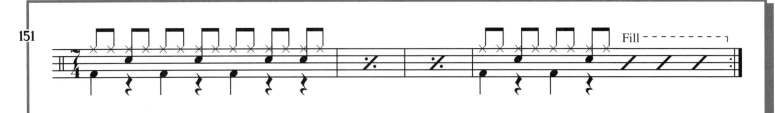

Three-Beat Fills

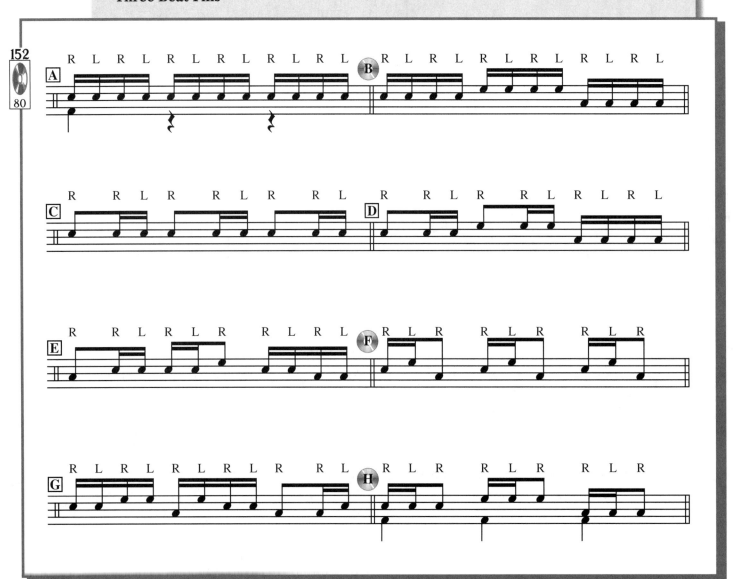

More Three-Beat Fills

Four-Bar Phrases

Four-Beat Fills

In the recorded versions of the following examples, a full measure of time playing will be heard before each "fill" measure.

Four-Bar Phrases

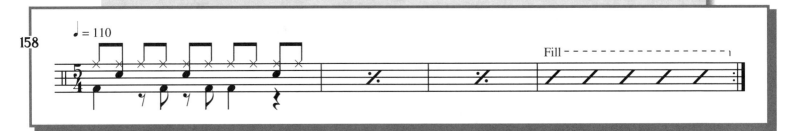

Five-Beat Fills

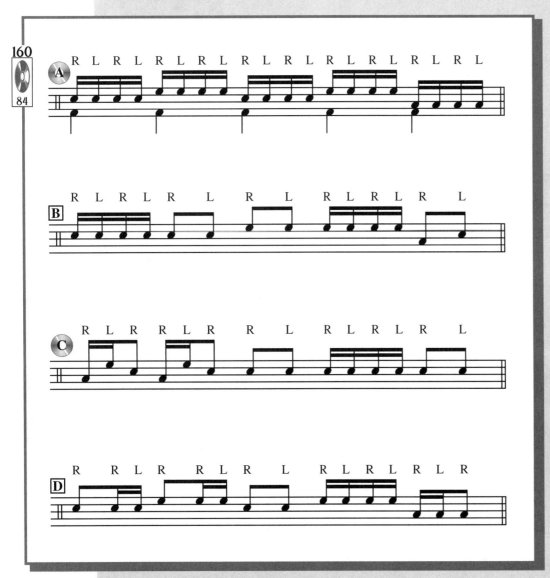

More Five-Beat Fills

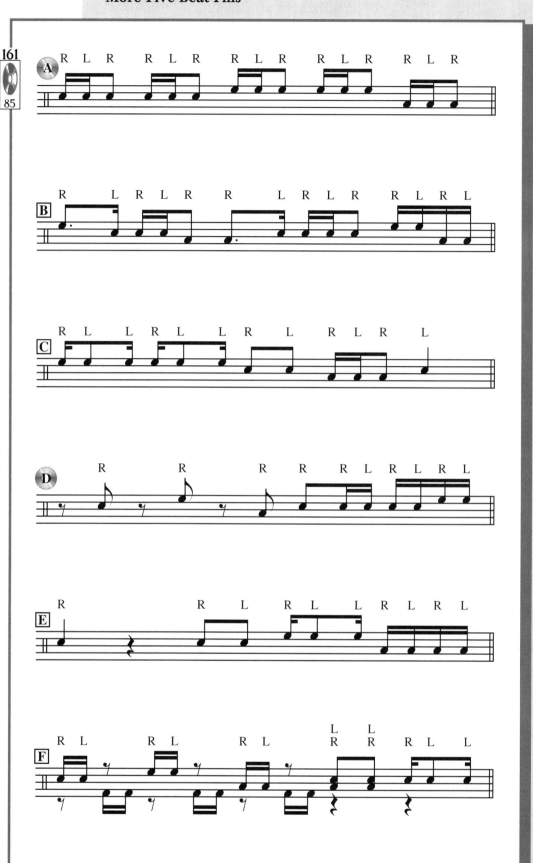

Now, we'll look at some six-beat and one-bar fill examples applied to $\frac{7}{4}$. Although fills of this length could be used to signal a musical transition, they are more likely to be played in a short solo break.

Four-Bar Phrase

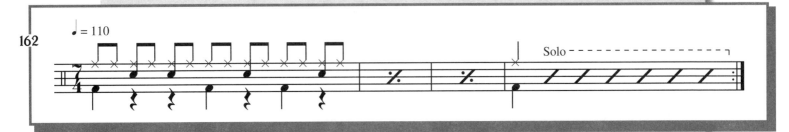

Six-Beat Fills/Solos

Four-Bar Phrase

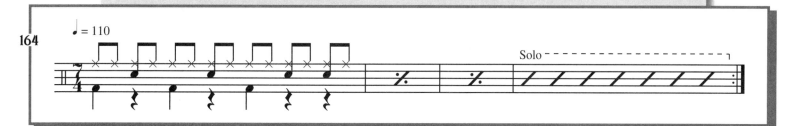

One-Bar Fills/Solos

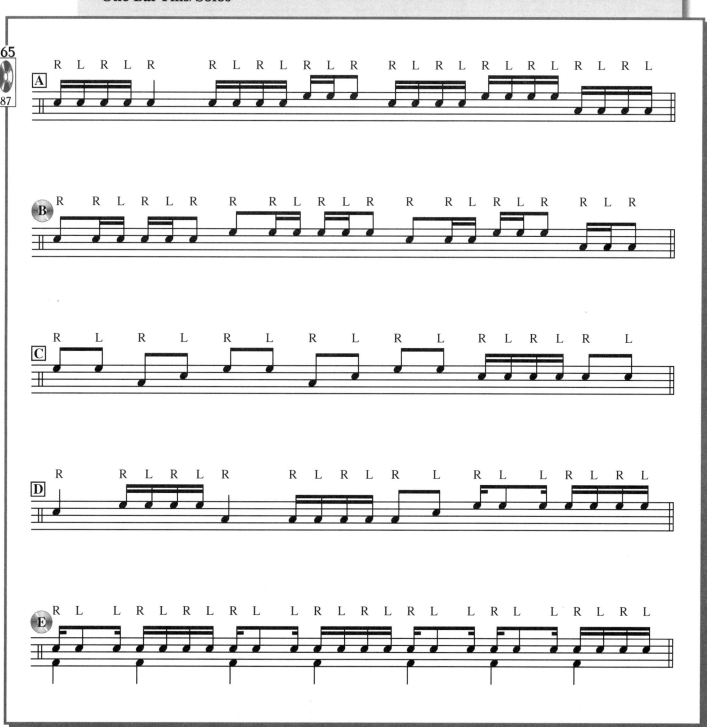

FILLS IN A SWING QUARTER-NOTE PULSE

Next up are fill ideas based on the triplet subdivision of a quarter-note pulse, in other words, swing time. These types of fills can be used in any style, but work particularly well in blues, country, and jazz. On the CD, you will hear only the last measure of $\frac{7}{4}$ with the included fill.

Four-Bar Phrases

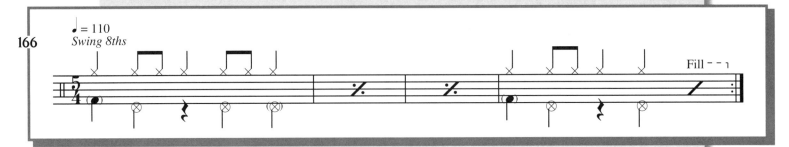

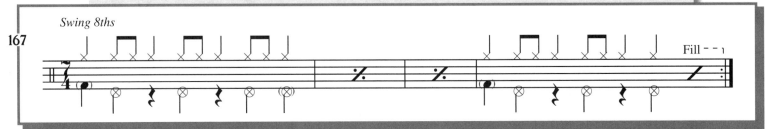

One-Beat Fills

Four-Bar Phrases

Two-Beat Fills

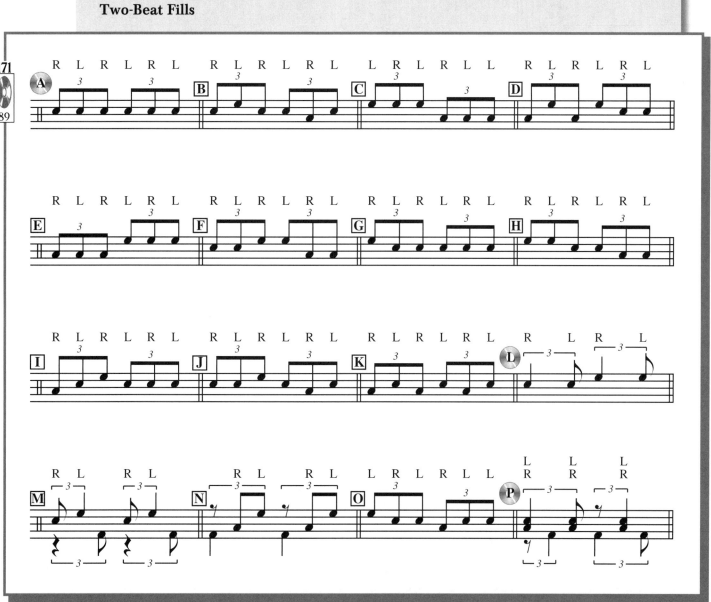

Four-Bar Phrases

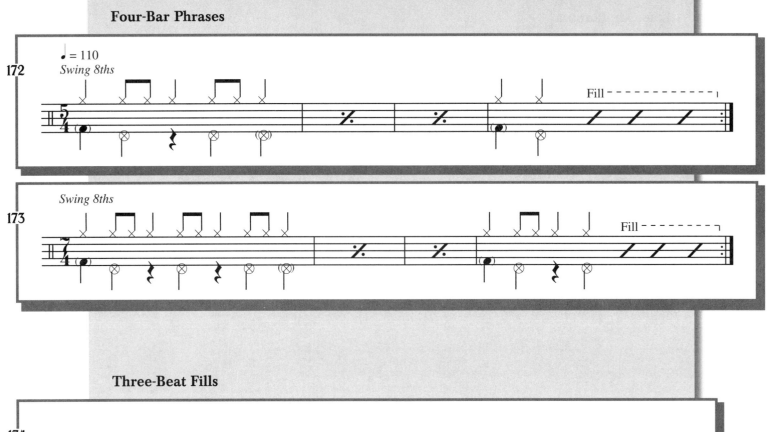

Three-Beat Fills

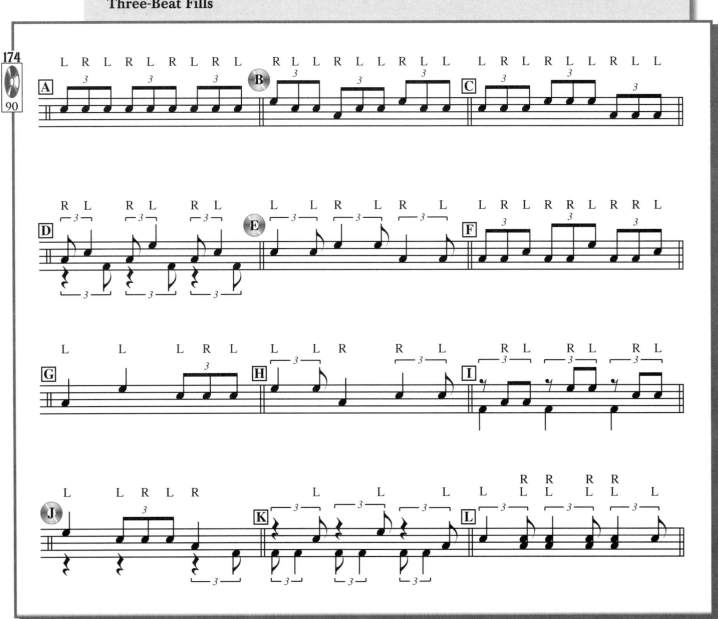

Four-Bar Phrases

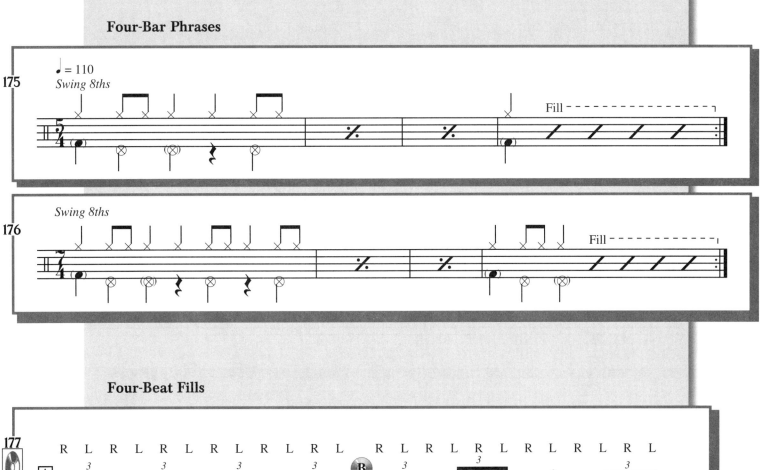

Four-Beat Fills

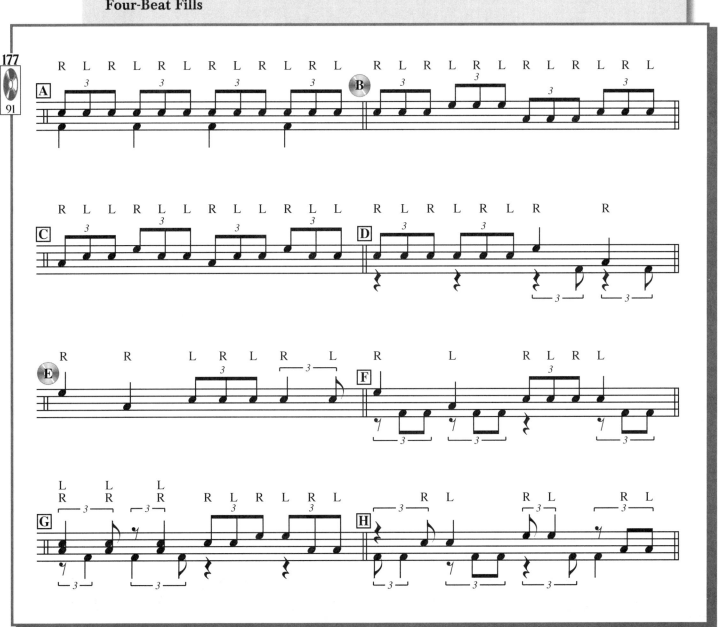

On the CD, the following examples will include a full measure of time playing before the fill measure.

Four-Bar Phrases

Five-Beat Fills

Now, we'll look at six-beat and one-bar fills in $\frac{7}{4}$. Remember, fills of this length more often than not are applied as short solo breaks rather than as a signal for a new section of the tune.

Four-Bar Phrase

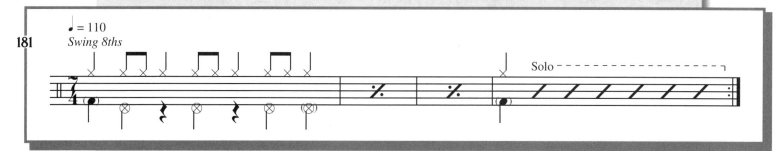

Six-Beat Fills/Solos

Four-Bar Phrase

One-Bar Fills/Solos

FILLS IN A DOTTED QUARTER-NOTE PULSE

Next, we will look at one-beat fill ideas based on eighth- and sixteenth-note subdivisions of a dotted quarter-note pulse. These will be used in the "eighth-note based" odd time signatures such as $\frac{5}{8}$ and $\frac{7}{8}$. On the CD, one full measure of time playing in $\frac{7}{8}$ will be heard before the measure with the fill.

Four-Bar Phrases

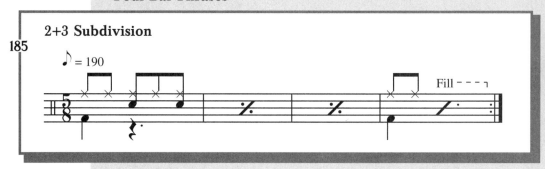

2+3 Subdivision

185

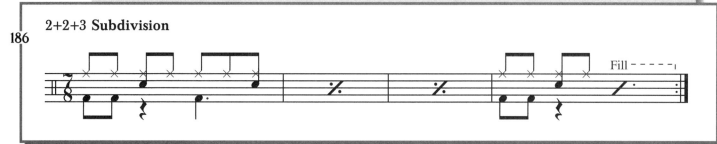

2+2+3 Subdivision

186

One-Beat (Dotted Quarter-Note) Fills

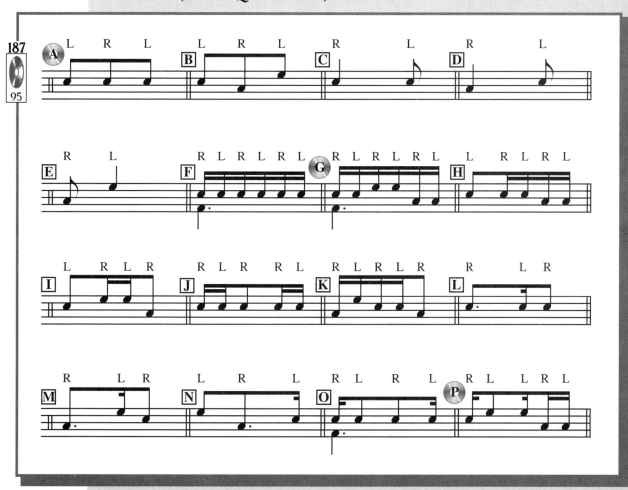

187

95

You can combine the examples from the previous page with the one-beat quarter-note examples from earlier in the chapter to create two-beat mixed-pulse fill ideas. (Remember, a mixed pulse is the combination of quarter-note and dotted quarter-note pulses.)

Four-Bar Phrases

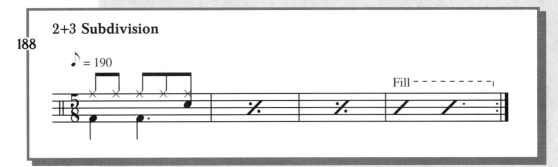

Two-Beat Mixed-Pulse Fills

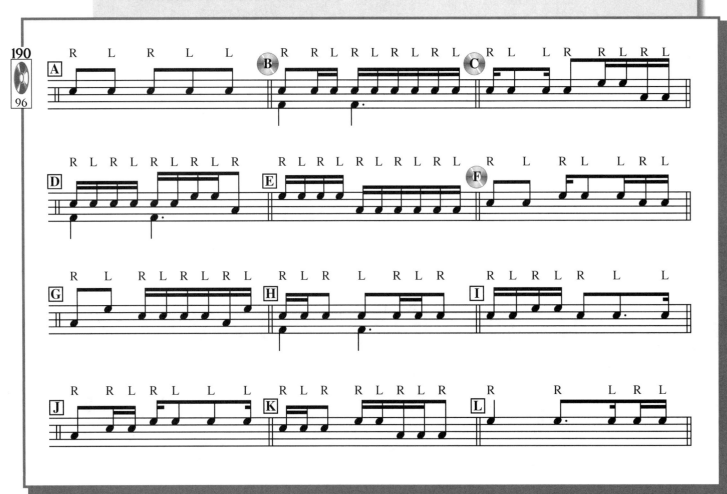

As you saw in the chapters on time playing, the biggest difference between odd time signatures, particularly "eighth-note" based time signatures ($\frac{5}{8}$, $\frac{7}{8}$, etc.), and $\frac{4}{4}$ is the variety of odd and even note groupings available. The examples on the previous page work as fill ideas for time signatures that end with (or are) a 2+3 subdivision. You can "flip" these types of ideas so that they start on the "three" (dotted quarter-note pulse). This will create 3+2 fill ideas.

Four-Bar Phrases

3+2 Subdivision

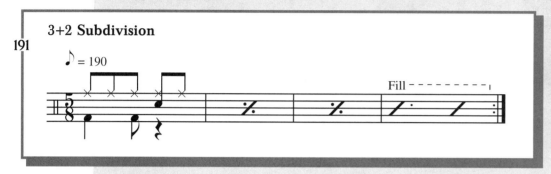

2+3+2 Subdivision

Two-Beat Mixed-Pulse Fills

Here are some one-bar fills in the two most common subdivisions of $\frac{7}{8}$: 2+2+3 and 3+2+2.

Four-Bar Phrase

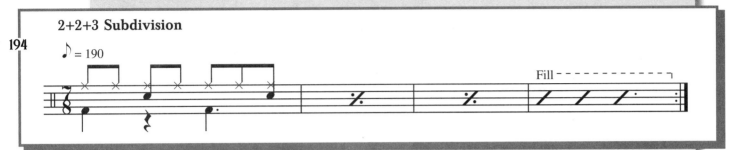

One-Bar Fills

Four-Bar Phrase

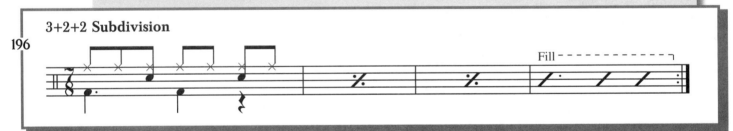

One-Bar Fills

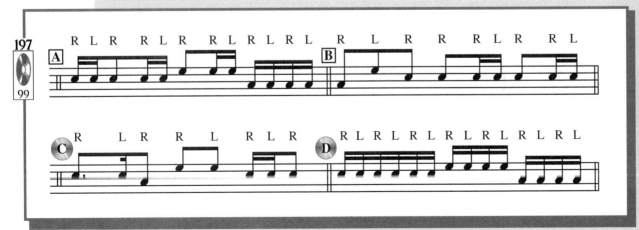

CONCLUSION

Having worked through this book, you should now have a better understanding of how to feel, hear, and play odd time signatures in a variety of styles. As mentioned throughout the book, the examples shown are just that—examples. They are intended to help you become comfortable with odd time signatures and the concepts of pulse, subdivisions, and note groupings. You are encouraged to experiment and discover variations of your own. This book should be used as a springboard for your own creativity.

Often, odd time signatures are applied to what might be referred to as "fusion" music. This is music where styles (sometimes several) are combined to create new styles and variations. Since the end result is not strictly traditional, there is plenty of room for experimentation. Try your best to be musical and not make odd time applications an intellectual exercise. The point is to make music and hopefully communicate with others. The most important tools you possess are your ears. Listen!

RECOMMENDED LISTENING

Following is a list of recordings that use odd time signatures. These are just the tip of the iceberg.

PROGRESSIVE ROCK AND RELATED

Genesis
- *Selling England by the Pound*
- *The Lamb Lies Down on Broadway*
- *A Trick of the Tail*

King Crimson
- *Lark's Tongues in Aspic*
- *Starless and Bible Black*
- *Discipline*
- *Beat*
- *Thrak*
- *The Power to Believe*

Bruford
- *One of a Kind*

Yes
- *Close to the Edge*

Rush
- *Moving Pictures*
- *Signals*

Tool
- *Lateralus*
- *10,000 Days*

Radiohead
- *Hail to the Thief*
- *In Rainbows*

Sting
- *Ten Summoner's Tales*
- *Mercury Falling*

JAZZ AND RELATED

Dave Brubeck Quartet
- *For All Time* box set (includes *Time Out, Time Further Out, Countdown, Time in Outer Space, Time Changes,* and *Time In)*

Don Ellis
- *Live at Monterey*
- *Electric Bath*

Bill Bruford's Earthworks
- *A Part, and Yet Apart*
- *The Sound of Surprise*

WORLD MUSIC AND WORLD FUSION MUSIC

Rabih Abou-Khalil
- *The Sultan's Picnic*
- *Blue Camel*

Yuri Yunakov (Bulgarian wedding music):
- Any recording

Ivo Papasov (Bulgarian wedding music)
- Any recording

Varttina
- Any recording

Pachora
- Any recording